CHILD EMOTIONAL SECURITY AND INTERPARENTAL CONFLICT

Patrick T. Davies
Gordon T. Harold
Marcie C. Goeke-Morey
E. Mark Cummings

IN COLLABORATION WITH
Katherine Shelton
Jennifer A. Rasi

WITH COMMENTARY BY
Jennifer M. Jenkins

Willis F. Overton
Series Editor

D1367545

Blackwell
Publishing

Boston, Massachusetts   Oxford, United Kingdom

CHILD EMOTIONAL SECURITY AND INTERPARENTAL CONFLICT

CONTENTS

COMMENTARY

ABSTRACT

Davies, Patrick T.; Harold, Gordon T., Goeke-Morey, Marcie C., and Cummings, E. Mark. Child Emotional Security and Interparental Conflict. *Monographs of the Society for Research in Child Development*, *2002*, **67** (3, Serial No. 270).

Guided by the emotional security hypothesis developed by Davies & Cummings (1994), studies were conducted to test a conceptual refinement of children's adjustment to parental conflict in relation to hypotheses of other prominent theories. Study 1 examined whether the pattern of child responses to simulations of adult conflict tactics and topics was consistent with the emotional security hypothesis and social learning theory in a sample of 327 Welsh children. Supporting the emotional security hypothesis, child reports of fear, avoidance, and involvement were especially prominent responses to destructive conflict.

Study 2 examined the relative roles of child emotional insecurity and social-cognitive appraisals in accounting for associations between parental conflict and child psychological symptoms in a sample of 285 Welsh children and parents. Findings indicated that child emotional insecurity was a robust intervening process in the prospective links between parental conflict and child maladjustment even when intervening processes proposed in the social-cognitive models were included in the analyses.

Studies 3 and 4 explored pathways among parental conflict, child emotional insecurity, and psychological adjustment in the broader family context with a sample of 174 children and mothers. Supporting the emotional security hypothesis, Study 3 findings indicated that child insecurity continued to mediate the link between parental conflict and child maladjustment even after specifying the effects of other parenting processes. Parenting difficulties accompanying interparental conflict were related to child maladjustment through their association with insecure parent-child attachment.

In support of the emotional security hypothesis, Study 4 findings indicated that family instability, parenting difficulties, and parent-child attachment insecurity potentiated mediational pathways among parental conflict, child insecurity, and maladjustment. Family cohesiveness, interparental satisfaction, and interparental expressiveness appeared to be protective factors in these mediational paths. No support was found for the social learning theory prediction that parent-child warmth would amplify associations between parental conflict and child disruptive behaviors.

I. INTRODUCTION AND LITERATURE REVIEW

Witnessing conflict between parents is a normal part of family life for children, especially when conflict is broadly defined as any dispute, disagreement, or difference of opinion (Cummings & Davies, 2002). Some forms of parental conflict (e.g., resolved) may have benign or salubrious consequences for family and child functioning. Yet, destructive ways of managing conflicts are also prevalent, as evidenced by the high rates of interparental dissolution and the statistics on the prevalence of conflict, violence, and dissatisfaction in intact marriages (Cummings & Davies, 1994; Hetherington, Bridges, & Insabella, 1998). Children are at risk for suffering adverse psychological consequences as bystanders to their parents' relationship difficulties. Exposure to high levels of interparental conflict increases the child's risk for a wide array of psychological problems, including emotional (e.g., depressive symptoms, anxiety), behavioral (e.g., aggression, delinquency), social (e.g., poor peer relations), and academic difficulties (e.g., Dunn & Davies, 2001; Erel & Burman, 1995; Grych & Fincham, 2001).

The assertion that marital quality is a key predictor of child maladjustment is not new (e.g., Hubbard & Adams, 1936; Towle, 1931). Although progress following this early work has established that interparental conflict is a better predictor of a wide range of child problems than many other aspects of marital quality (e.g., satisfaction, distress), simply replicating associations between interparental conflict and child adjustment has reached a point of diminishing returns (Grych & Fincham, 2001). In response, researchers are now pursuing a second generation of process-oriented research on interparental conflict (Fincham, 1994). A fundamental aim of this new generation of research is to precisely delineate the processes and conditions that are responsible for the association between interparental conflict and children's psychological functioning.

Process models are designed to provide answers to two main sets of questions. First, mediational models are a subclass of process models that attempt to determine *how* or *why* a particular factor, such as interparental

1

conflict, poses a risk for child adjustment. Mediators are the *generative mechanisms* through which independent variables affect outcomes (Baron & Kenny, 1986; Holmbeck, 1997). Thus, within the parental conflict literature, the new generation of research has involved identifying the mechanisms and processes that explain how and why interparental conflict is associated with forms of child maladjustment like internalizing (e.g., depression, anxiety, social withdrawal) and externalizing (e.g., aggression, delinquency) symptoms. Analytically, identifying a mediator requires demonstrating that a focal variable accounts for substantial amounts of variance in the link between interparental conflict and child maladjustment.

Second, moderator models are a subclass of process models that address the question of *when* the risk factor is most or least likely to be associated with a particular outcome. Moderators specify the strength and/or direction of relations between an independent variable (e.g., interparental conflict) and a dependent variable (e.g., child adjustment) (Baron & Kenny, 1986; Holmbeck, 1997). Protective factors are moderators that, at high levels, reduce the association between interparental conflict and child maladjustment. For example, the association between interparental conflict and child maladjustment may be substantially reduced when children experience warm parent-child relations and family cohesiveness. Conversely, potentiating factors are moderators that amplify the risk posed by marital conflict. For example, links between interparental conflict and child psychological problems may be substantially stronger in depressive or alcoholic families (Cummings & Davies, 2002; El-Sheikh & Flanagan, 2001). Analytically, demonstrating moderation requires that the magnitude of the association between interparental conflict and child maladjustment differ significantly at high and low levels of the proposed moderator.

Process models of interparental conflict have been especially valuable in highlighting key themes of the second generation of research, particularly in (a) delineating how interrelations between interparental conflict and child functioning vary as a function of different conflict characteristics, (b) identifying the processes that interparental conflict may set in motion within the child which increase vulnerability to adjustment problems (i.e., intrachild mediators), (c) explicating the specific processes in the family that may account for the risk posed by interparental conflict (i.e., family mediators), and (d) identifying the family characteristics that may reduce or amplify the relationship between interparental conflict and child functioning (i.e., moderators) (Cummings & Davies, 2002). Davies and Cummings (1994) developed a model, called the *emotional security hypothesis,* to serve as a heuristic or guide in addressing these process-oriented questions. According to this theory, interparental conflict increases the child's vulnerability to psychological problems by threatening his or her sense of security in multiple family contexts (e.g., inter-

2

parental, parent-child). Consistent with process-oriented themes, the aims of the emotional security hypothesis specifically consist of (a) identifying the parameters of interparental conflict that are associated with the child's difficulties in preserving emotional security; (b) examining the role that the child's security (i.e., intrachild process) plays in accounting for pathways among interparental conflict and child maladjustment; (c) explicating mediational pathways between interparental conflict, the child's security, and adjustment within the larger context of other family mediators (e.g., parenting); and (d) identifying characteristics in the larger family system that may alter the magnitude or nature of emotional security as a mediator of parental conflict.

This *Monograph* presents the results of studies designed to further develop and test a model of emotional security and interparental conflict by systematically addressing these four themes. Although the original formulation of the emotional security hypothesis highlighted the importance of pursuing these questions, the early stage of theory and research hindered the development of a theoretically guided set of clear, precise hypotheses (Davies & Cummings, 1994). Thus, our first aim in the present research was to advance a more refined, updated conceptualization of emotional security in the context of interparental conflict. Particular emphasis was placed on refining the conceptual account to permit more precise empirical tests. To bridge the gap between conceptual and empirical advances, our second goal was to empirically test theoretically guided hypotheses about the child's emotional security in the face of interparental conflict.

In addressing these two goals, we specifically sought to test hypotheses derived from the emotional security hypothesis in relation to hypotheses derived from complementary theories of interparental conflict. Our contention was that progress in understanding why the child is affected by interparental conflict will require consideration of multiple processes derived from diverse theoretical frameworks. The second generation of research has already yielded considerable gains in developing and refining several other conceptual models of the processes accounting for the relationship between interparental conflict and child adjustment. For example, a recent review identified several general classes of theories that offer explanations for why interparental conflict poses a risk for the child (Margolin, Oliver, & Medina, 2001). Although empirical research has also moved to the level of identifying the processes that account for the risk of interparental conflict, it has, on balance, lagged behind theory. Findings from many studies are interpreted as supporting various theories in a post hoc manner (Emery, 1982). Likewise, among the handful of studies that were guided by a priori theoretical considerations, most, if not all, are limited to testing explanatory mechanisms derived from a single theory in isolation from processes formulated by other theories. Thus, little is known about the interplay among and relative role of processes outlined in different theories. The goal of the investigation presented in this *Monograph* is to provide a more authoritative test of why marital conflict increases the child's vulnerability to psychological difficulties by examining the role of mechanisms proposed by the emotional security hypothesis in relation to mechanisms described by alternative theories of interparental conflict.

In this chapter we outline the theoretical details of the emotional security hypothesis. We also describe the main assumptions of three prominent, alternative theories of interparental conflict, with an eye toward delineating how the assumptions and predictions from our theory differ from these other theories. Particular emphasis is then placed on further refining, clarifying, and explicating the primary assumptions of the emotional security hypothesis and the conceptual bases underlying the four themes for advancing an understanding of the child's emotional security in the family.

In Chapters II–V we present four studies designed to test the emotional security hypothesis in relation to hypotheses derived from these alternative models. As products of collaborative relations among researchers at the University of Rochester, the University of Notre Dame, and Cardiff University (Wales), these studies were designed to authoritatively address a programmatic, interlocking set of aims and hypotheses derived from the emotional security hypothesis (Cummings & Davies, 1996; Davies & Cummings, 1994). For each study, we specifically present the conceptualization and focal hypotheses, methods, results, and discussion. Finally, Chapter VI is designed to integrate the main findings across the *Monograph*, especially in relation to refining the emotional security hypothesis in the context of other theoretical models and outlining directions for future research.

THE EMOTIONAL SECURITY HYPOTHESIS

The original emotional security hypothesis was directed toward developing bases for hypothesizing that the child's emotional insecurity mediates the link between interparental conflict and child maladjustment (Cummings & Davies, 1996; Davies & Cummings, 1994). Thus, a primary message of these early accounts was that exposure to interparental conflict increased the child's risk for adjustment problems through its association with three main signs of insecurity: high levels of emotional reactivity, forms of regulating exposure to parent affect, and negative internal representations of interparental relations. Despite its heuristic value in the literature, we believe that the subsequent viability of the emotional security hypothesis hinges on further conceptual refinement and reformulation in both precision and scope. At the level of precision, the original emotional security hypothesis described emotional security as a goal within a larger control system (e.g., Davies & Cummings, 1994), but it was decidedly vague about the operation of this system in the context of interparental conflict, and the interplay between the latent goal of emotional security and the three component processes comprising the system. The resulting lack of theoretical specificity has led to particular difficulty in developing methodological tools and designs to permit empirical testing of key hypotheses. To increase the precision of the theory, our first goal in refining the emotional security hypothesis was to more precisely specify the nature of this control system and its methodological implications. As part of this revision, we distinguish between the short-term and long-term adaptational functions of the mechanisms (e.g., emotional reactivity, internal representations, regulation of exposure to parent affect) comprising the goal-corrected system of emotional security.

With respect to scope, our original theoretical account was primarily confined to the relationship between interparental conflict styles and child emotional security in the context of interparental conflict. Thus, despite acknowledging the importance of developing a family-wide model of emotional security, the review failed to systematically address two key classes of variables necessary to build a broader family model. First, it did not specify how an interpersonal constellation of factors in the family system may play a role in further clarifying the nature of associations between interparental conflict and the child's emotional security in the context of interparental conflict. Second, it did not articulate how the goal of preserving emotional security is interrelated to control systems of emotional security in other close family relationships (e.g., parent-child attachment). For example, if the child's emotional security in the face of parental conflict is distinct from security in the parent-child attachment relationship as our theory proposes, are these forms of insecurity related to different aspects of family functioning? Or do they share a common set of family correlates? How might emotional security in the context of various family relationships be collectively related to child adjustment? To increase the scope, the second aim of our conceptual refinement was to place the control system of emotional security, as it operates in the context of interparental conflict, within a broader family systems framework. By increasing the precision and scope, we hope to further the second generation of family research by elucidating (a) the multiple mediating pathways through which interparental and family difficulties are linked with child adjustment, and (b) the family and child characteristics that play a role in the risk posed by interparental difficulties.

The emotional security hypothesis posits that preserving a sense of security is an important *goal* that organizes a child's emotional experiences (e.g., fear), action tendencies (e.g., withdraw, intervene), and appraisals of self and interpersonal relationships (e.g., perceptions of threat to the self). Although the child evaluates interpersonal contexts in relation to multiple goals, the emotional security hypothesis postulates that protection, safety, and security are among the most salient and important goals in the hierarchy of human goals (see Crockenberg & Langrock, 2001a for a discussion of other goals). Theorists have long underscored the significance of emotional security in accounts of normal development and the development of psychopathology (e.g., Ainsworth, Blehar, Waters, & Wall, 1978; Blatz, 1966; Bowlby, 1969; Cummings & Cicchetti, 1990; Waters & Cummings, 2000). Consistent with attachment theory, the emotional security hypothesis is a developmental theory that accepts the notion that the child's emotional security can be enhanced or undermined by the quality of parent-child relations. The theories also share the assumption that the child's success in preserving security has long-term implications for psychological adjustment (Bretherton, Ridgeway, & Cassidy, 1990; Thompson, 2000).

However, the emotional security hypothesis differs from attachment theory in positing that the child's emotional security is a significant goal across multiple family relationships. In the new conceptualization, the goal of preserving security is also postulated to be salient for the child in the *context* of the interparental relationship difficulties, especially during bouts of parental conflict. Thus, in our theory, the interparental relationship is a contextual factor that may enhance or undermine the child's security in parent-child contexts. But, more important, we propose that the child also develops a sense of security in the context of interparental conflict that is distinct from security experienced in parent-child contexts (e.g., attachment). Thus, the child may be insecure in the interparental context but secure in parent-child contexts or vice versa. Moreover, the assumption is that emotional security in the context of interparental conflict has unique implications for child developmental outcomes even in the context of parent-child attachment security.

The child has sound reasons for being distinctly concerned with interparental conflict and discord. For example, parental discord may undermine the child's security by signifying a loved one's unhappiness and emotional instability and raising the possibility of family dissolution (e.g., divorce) and its accompanying hardships. The child may also fear that distressed parents may become emotionally unresponsive or carry unresolved hostility from marital conflicts into parent-child interactions. It follows then that the child may be especially concerned about security when conflict characteristics are likely to result in adversity in the larger family system. Thus, Path 1 of Figure 1 is presented to illustrate that witnessing conflict characterized by intense anger expression, escalating hostility, and discordant endings is especially likely to sensitize the child to concerns about the goal of preserving his or her security (Cummings & Davies, 1996; Davies & Cummings, 1994).

Emotional security is conceptualized as a latent goal that can be inferred from three observable classes of response processes (i.e., component processes). Signs of insecurity in the face of interparental discord are specifically reflected in (a) emotional reactivity, characterized by intense, prolonged, and dysregulated distress (e.g., fear, vigilance) reactions to interparental conflict; (b) regulation of exposure to parent affect, as evidenced by prolonged, rigid attempts to become involved in or avoid parental conflict; and (c) internal representations of interparental relations, as indexed by the child's evaluations of the potential consequences parental conflict has for his or her well-being. Thus, according to the emotional security hypothesis, the child who experiences prolonged histories of exposure to destructive conflict will experience greater insecurity as inferred by greater emotional reactivity, avoidance and involvement, and hostile representations in the context of interparental conflict.

The Interplay Between Security and the Three Component Processes

A puzzling theoretical question still remains: Why would a child from a high conflict home manifest greater distress, rigid and extreme forms of regulating exposure to parent affect, and negative expectancies or representations? Why, for example, would he or she not habituate or get used to the fact that parents fight a lot and have many intense, disruptive disagreements? After all, experiencing high levels of reactivity to conflict is unpleasant and may jeopardize the child's functioning in the long run. The emotional security hypothesis suggests that it may be adaptive for the child to respond in this way in the interparental and family context. Path 2 in Figure 1 is presented to underscore that emotional security is a control system in which the goal of security regulates and is regulated by three component processes. Thus, the goal of regaining or preserving emotional security is thought to precipitate responding across the component processes. The three component processes of emotional security, in turn, are conceptualized as biologically rooted vehicles that were originally designed to procure physical and psychological protection and, hence, security.

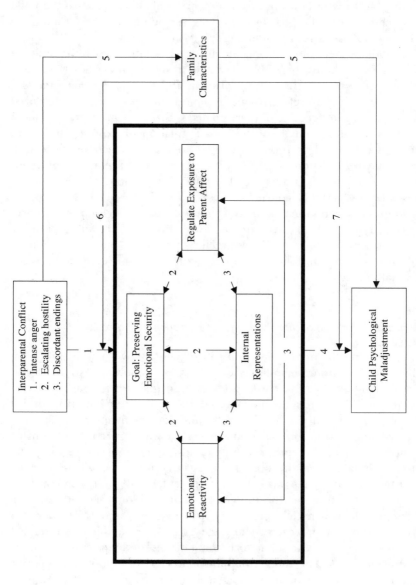

FIGURE 1.—A family-wide model of the impact of interparental conflict on child emotional security and psychological adjustment.

Emotional reactivity. Earlier conceptualizations of the emotional security hypothesis were relatively vague about which specific emotional experiences were the most reliable signs of insecurity (Davies & Cummings, 1994). For example, Crockenberg and Langrock (2001a) noted that early predictions and tests of the emotional security hypothesis failed to distinguish between specific emotions in assessing emotional reactivity (e.g., Davies & Cummings, 1998; Davies, Myers, Cummings, & Heindel, 1999). As a result, emotions such as fear, anger, and sadness were given relatively equal weight as signs of insecurity. Although we still argue that several types of affect can reflect insecurity (e.g., sadness, anger), our updated account proposes that greater concerns about preserving security are especially likely to prime the child's fear and vigilance. Greater negative emotional reactivity, in turn, helps in reattaining emotional security. By increasing accessibility to identifying, processing, and recalling negative, aversive events (Davies & Cummings, 1995; 1998; Terwogt, Kremer, & Stegge, 1991), tendencies to experience fear and vigilance may help to emotionally tag or underscore potential sources of threat that commonly accompany conflicts between distressed parents. The physiological and emotional arousal generated from fearful and vigilant reactions to conflict may simultaneously increase the availability of physical and psychological resources for coping and defending against potential threats accompanying parental conflict (Saarni, Mumme, & Campos, 1998; Thompson & Calkins, 1996). Thus, although experiencing greater distress and vigilance is inherently negative and unpleasant, it may have short-term adaptive value in protecting the well-being of a child who has experienced a history of destructive parental conflict.

Despite having some adaptive function, tendencies to experience emotional reactivity in response to conflict do reflect at two levels the difficulties in preserving security. At one level, dispositions toward experiencing fear and distress in reaction to conflict reflect greater activation of the goal of preserving security. Likewise, at another level of analysis, difficulties modulating or recovering from distress signify continued difficulties regaining security. In support of this notion, research using a variety of methodologies (e.g., diary, survey, observational, experimental-analogue) has demonstrated that prolonged exposure to destructive interparental conflict (e.g., intense, escalating, violent, unresolved) engenders progressively more negative emotional reactions to subsequent conflicts (e.g., Cummings, Goeke-Morey, Papp, & Dukewich, in press; Davies & Cummings, 1998; Davies et al., 1999; El-Sheikh, 1997; Gordis, Margolin, & John, 1997).

Internal representations. As another sign of child insecurity, negative internal representations are theorized to increase with greater exposure to parental conflict. An understanding of the function of representations in the emotional security system requires a description of our conceptualization of internal representations. In our theory, internal representations do not simply reflect the child's analysis of the frequency or physical characteristics of conflict. Rather, the child analyzes the implications that interparental conflict has for preserving or undermining his or her sense of security. Of particular relevance to the child's sense of security are the analyses of the consequences that interparental conflict has for the child's own well-being (e.g., worries of spillover of spousal hostilities to the parent-child relationship, divorce) and attachment figures in the family (e.g., fears conflict will escalate or irreparably damage the interparental relationship). Actively processing the meaning of parental conflict at this higher order level is thought to help children from high conflict homes protect themselves because the processing may serve as a cognitive map or alarm for identifying interparental events that may eventually proliferate to undermine the welfare of the self and family (Thompson, Flood, & Lundquist, 1995). Thus, hostile representational systems primed to the possibility of danger (e.g., pessimistic expectancies regarding the outcome of parental conflicts) may help children from high conflict homes gain security by enhancing their ability to proactively protect themselves and their family. In support of this hypothesis, interparental conflict histories predict more hostile representations of the harmful implications parental difficulties have for the welfare of the self and family (e.g., Davies & Cummings, 1998; Grych, 1998; Grych, Fincham, Jouriles, & MacDonald, 2000; Harold & Conger, 1997; Harold, Fincham, Osborne, & Conger, 1997).

Regulation of exposure to parent affect. The goal of preserving security also serves an organizing function by guiding the child to regulate his or her exposure to stressful parental emotion. Insecurity is specifically thought to increase the child's efforts to become involved in or to avoid the parental conflicts. These coping strategies are theorized to reflect attempts to control parental emotionality and behaviors before they escalate and result in more serious, negative consequences for the family (Cummings & Davies, 1996). Because interparental conflict in discordant homes is more likely to continue for long periods, get progressively worse, and spill over to affect other family members, attempts to mediate or avoid the conflict may help the child from a high conflict home regain security by reducing exposure to the threatening interparental event.

Studies examining relations between parental conflict, forms of regulating exposure to parent affect, and child adjustment have yielded inconsistent findings. For example, some findings indicate that children from high conflict homes exhibit heightened levels of intervention (Cummings, Hennessy, Rabideau, & Cicchetti, 1994; J.S. Cummings, Pellegrini, Notarius, & Cummings, 1989; Davies et al., 2002; Jenkins, Smith, & Graham,

1989; O'Brien, Margolin, John, & Krueger, 1991) and avoidance strategies (Davies, Forman, Rasi, & Stevens, 2002; Garcia O'Hearn, Margolin, & John, 1997) in coping with conflict, whereas other studies have reported complex or nonsignificant associations (Davies & Cummings, 1998; Gordis et al., 1997; Ingoldsby, Shaw, Owens, & Winslow, 1999; O'Brien, Bahadur, Gee, Balto, & Erber, 1997; O'Brien, Margolin, & John, 1995). However, inconsistency in the findings may be attributable, in large part, to inconsistencies in the operationalization and assessment of intervention and avoidance (Kerig, 2001). Consistent with this analysis, the emotional security hypothesis underscores that the substance and quality of the regulation strategy, rather than the mere presence, is the most accurate barometer of insecurity. Thus, although expending resources toward regulating exposure to conflict may serve as a sign that the goal of preserving security is activated, multiple prolonged attempts at intervening (e.g., comforting and role reversal as opposed to simply watching the dispute) or avoiding (e.g., freezing or hastily fleeing as opposed to distracting oneself through play), which require high levels of emotional and psychological risk or investment, are predicted to signify prolonged difficulties in regaining security.

Correspondence Among the Component Processes

Given that each of the three component processes is conceptualized as serving the same goal of preserving security, the bidirectional arrows in Path 3 of Figure 1 are presented to underscore that there should be some degree of interdependency among emotional reactivity, internal representations, and regulation of exposure to parent affect. By the same token, each of the components or classes of responses is assumed to represent a distinct aspect of the emotional security system. Thus, consistent with an organizational perspective on the functioning of regulatory systems of emotional security (Cummings & Davies, 1996; Sroufe & Waters, 1977), striving to reach the goal of security may be manifested in myriad ways. That is, component processes reflecting failure or difficulty in achieving emotional security do not necessarily occur in unison, as insecurity may surface in any number of response domains (e.g., overt distress, subjective distress, avoidance or involvement, negative representations).

Accordingly, rather than predicting a one-to-one correspondence among components, the emotional security hypothesis postulates that the concrete indicators reflecting insecurity will evidence modest to moderate interrelations. In accord with this hypothesis, earlier studies have reported moderate to modest correlations among the indices of emotional reactivity, regulation of exposure to parent affect, and internal representations (Davies & Cummings, 1998; Davies et al., 2002). Thus, increases in emotional reactivity are expected to be associated with greater efforts to regulate exposure to parent affect (i.e., avoidance, involvement) and more negative appraisals of interparental relations. Likewise, reductions in signs of insecurity in one response domain (i.e., regulation of exposure to parent affect) are theorized to be associated with decreases in insecurity in the remaining response domains (e.g., diminished emotional reactivity, more positive internal representations).

Implications of Child Security for Long-Term Adjustment

Although preserving emotional security may initially be adaptive in preserving the well-being of the child, the theory further postulates that, in the long run, it is maladaptive for the child's psychological adjustment (see Path 4, Figure 1). Vigilance, fear, and preoccupation with complicated adult problems are thought to increase the child's risk for more pervasive psychological difficulties, including internalizing and externalizing symptoms (Davies et al., 2002; Grych, Fincham, et al., 2000). Likewise, insecure children may be especially likely to use their pessimistic expectancies or representations of the aftermath of parental conflict as a guide in interpreting or understanding other challenging or novel contexts (e.g., peer relations, school). Tendencies to respond in rigid, maladaptive ways in these new settings may, over time, crystallize into forms of maladjustment that persist across time and setting. By the same token, the child who experiences secure appraisals of the interparental relationship is posited to (a) be more flexible, open, and skilled in forming and maintaining social relationships and (b) learn important social lessons on how to approach interpersonal disputes in constructive ways. Thus, indicators of security are hypothesized to be associated with greater psychological adjustment.

Frequent and prolonged operation of the emotional security system also requires considerable expenditure of psychological and physical resources to regulate attention, affect, thought processes, and action tendencies. Thus, the energy expended to regain security may subsequently limit the resources a child needs to pursue other significant developmental goals. As a result, the child who experiences frequent and prolonged bouts of insecurity may be at increased risk for exhibiting psychological symptoms (Saarni et al., 1998; Thompson & Calkins, 1996). Consistent with this hypothesis, studies have shown that indices of emotional insecurity (i.e., negative emotional reactivity, involvement, avoidance, negative internal representations) are significantly related to child internalizing symptoms, externalizing problems, and other forms of psychological maladjustment (e.g., Davies & Cummings, 1998; Harold et al., 1997; O'Brien et al., 1997). Conversely, the child who is able to efficiently preserve a sense of security in the face of interparental adversity may have the luxury of expending higher levels of psychological and physical resources to master other developmental tasks (e.g., social competence, emotion regulation).

Interparental Conflict and Child Security in the Broader Family Context

Interparental conflict and child coping and adjustment are closely intertwined with other family characteristics (e.g., parenting practices, family cohesion, parent-child relations). Individual differences in child experiences in other aspects of the family context may specifically alter mediational pathways among interparental conflict history, child insecurity, and child maladjustment. Thus, it is difficult to draw any definitive conclusions about emotional security as a mediator of interparental conflict without more fully integrating these models in the larger family system.

From the perspective of the emotional security hypothesis (Cummings & Davies, 1995; Davies & Cummings, 1994), other family experiences may influence the mediating role of emotional security through two pathways. Path 5 of Figure 1 is presented to underscore a first type of pathway in which characteristics of the family system outside of interparental processes are theorized to mediate the associations between interparental conflict and child adjustment. Research testing these *indirect effects models* has specifically shown that parenting practices such as parental hostility, rejection, and lax monitoring account for part of the association between interparental conflict and child adjustment (e.g., Gonzalez, Pitts, Hill, & Roosa, 2000; Miller, Cowan, Cowan, Hetherington, & Clingempeel, 1993; Stocker & Youngblade, 1999). In taking the indirect effects model one step further in the specification of process relations, the emotional security hypothesis proposes that parenting disturbances associated with interparental difficulties may also increase the child's risk for maladjustment by undermining their parent-child attachment security. Thus, interparental conflict may increase the child's vulnerability to maladjustment through two primary channels: (a) indirectly through its association with parenting difficulties and parent-child attachment insecurity, and (b) directly through its effect on the child's security in the context of interparental conflict.

Paths 6 and 7 in Figure 1 are presented to illustrate a second type of pathway involving family characteristics. Mediational pathways between interparental conflict, child emotional security, and psychological adjustment are specifically proposed to vary as a function of family characteristics. Path 6 is designed to show that family characteristics may either potentiate or protect the child from experiencing insecurity in the face of high levels of parental conflict. Difficulties in the larger family system may specifically potentiate the risk of interparental conflict by heightening the child's sensitivity and reactivity to conflict. According to the emotional security hypothesis, the child is especially likely to regard interparental conflict as a threat to security when it takes place in a distressed or unstable family. On the other hand, parental conflict may have minimal implications for the child who experiences supportive or cohesive family relationships. For example, experiencing warm, cohesive family relationships may buffer children from the threat parental conflict poses to their sense of security.

Path 7 in Figure 1 is presented to underscore that family characteristics may moderate the second link in the mediational pathway or, more specifically, the relationship between emotional security and child symptomatology. Family characteristics reflecting warmth and supportiveness (e.g., family cohesiveness) may provide the child with the psychological strengths and resources necessary to successfully cope with the insecurity and, as a result, reduce vulnerability to experiencing broader psychological problems. Conversely, forms of family adversity are posited to compound insecure children's vulnerability to psychological problems by further undermining their ability to utilize resources and skills necessary to successfully resolve important developmental tasks and sustain adaptive strategies for coping with challenges.

ALTERNATIVE THEORIES OF INTERPARENTAL CONFLICT

To examine the viability of the emotional security hypothesis, we specifically tested its hypotheses within the context of alternative, plausible hypotheses derived from three other major theories. Several important theories have emerged in the interparental conflict literature that merit serious consideration (e.g., Crockenberg & Langrock, 2001a, 2001b; Jenkins, 2000; Wilson & Gottman, 1995). However, in keeping with the aims of this *Monograph*, we limit our coverage to three theories: the social learning theory (Bandura, 1973), the cognitive-contextual framework (Grych & Fincham, 1990), and the indirect effects models (Fauber & Long, 1991). Selection of these three theories was guided by several considerations. First, these conceptualizations have all played leading roles in the research and the interpretation of findings throughout the second generation of research (Margolin et al., 2001). Second, these theories provide clear and precise bases for formulating hypotheses. Third, the behavioral, social-cognitive, and family processes of central concern to the social learning theory, the cognitive-contextual framework, and the indirect effects model, respectively, can be readily compared and contrasted with the processes outlined in the emotional security hypothesis. Accordingly, the following sections address some of the primary assumptions and derivative hypotheses of these complementary theories.

Social Learning Theory

Explanations derived from Albert Bandura's social learning theory emphasize how the child's responses are learned in the context of interparental interactions. Social learning theory shares some general similarities with emotional security in proposing that child exposure to interparental conflict tactics has direct effects on child functioning that cannot be accounted for by parenting. However, the specific assumptions and hypotheses about how interparental conflict affects the child's immediate functioning differ from the predictions of the emotional security hypothesis in important and empirically testable ways. According to social learning theory (Bandura, 1973; 1983), observational learning or modeling is regarded as even more influential in organizing the child's responses than are direct reinforcement or punishment contingencies. In the context of interparental conflict, the child masters new ways of engaging in aggressive behavior by vicariously observing adults engage in aggressive or hostile tactics. The child may exhibit greater hostility and aggression when exposed to more aggressive conflict tactics between adults through (a) precise imitation of specific hostile behaviors displayed by the discordant adults, (b) acquisition of generalized scripts or abstract rules for engaging in hostile behaviors, or (c) reduction of inhibitions about aggressing (Cox, Paley, & Harter, 2001; Cummings & Davies, 1995; Emery, 1982; Margolin et al., 2001). Consequently, a key hypothesis is that the child should experience more angry and aggressive reactions with exposure to progressively more aggressive conflict tactics displayed by adults (Graham-Bermann, 1998).

Social learning theory presupposes that modeling processes vary in strength depending on the degree to which the child readily identifies with and values potential adult models. The match between the gender of the child and parent is one condition that may be associated with the child's likelihood of identifying with and emulating potential models. Children are proposed to be more likely to model the behaviors of the same-sex parent than the opposite-sex parent (Emery, 1982; Johnson & O'Leary, 1987), as they incorporate gender-relevant scripts into their identities by early school-age and use gender as a basis for selecting which parental behaviors to imitate during bouts of interparental conflict (see Crockenberg & Langrock, 2001a; Davies & Lindsay, 2001). The derivative hypothesis is that boys are expected to be more likely to imitate or model the angry or aggressive behaviors of fathers than of mothers, and girls are

15

expected to be more likely to imitate or model the angry or aggressive behaviors of mothers than of fathers (Crockenberg & Langrock, 2001b).

The quality of the relationship between parent and child is proposed to be another important moderator in the modeling process. A basic premise of social learning theory is that children will also more readily imitate behaviors when they have warm and close relationships with the adults (Bandura & Walters, 1959; also see Andrews, Hops, & Duncan, 1997). Thus, from a social learning theory perspective, it is also hypothesized that the concordance between parental and child hostility will be substantially stronger for children who have warm, close relationships with their parents.

Modeling processes have long been influential as explanations for findings in the interparental conflict literature. Consistent associations between interparental conflict and the child's hostile, aggressive functioning have been frequently interpreted as providing evidence for social learning theory explanations (e.g., Crockenberg & Langrock, 2001a; Emery & O'Leary, 1982; Johnson & O'Leary, 1987). However, modeling explanations for general associations between interparental and child behavior are typically provided post hoc (Emery, 1982). These studies commonly fail to identify and test specific, empirical hypotheses that distinguish social learning theory from other theories. Moreover, empirical support for moderator hypotheses in the links between interparental and child behaviors has been inconsistent. For example, although some evidence suggests that boys' and girls' behaviors are more strongly associated with the conflict behaviors of the same-sex parent (e.g., Crockenberg & Langrock, 2001a; Johnson & O'Leary, 1987), other research on the moderating effects of parent and child gender have yielded null or contradictory findings (e.g., Crockenberg & Forgays, 1996; Davies & Lindsay, 2001; Katz & Gottman, 1993). Likewise, the association between some forms of parent and adolescent aversive behaviors (e.g., substance use) have been shown to be significantly stronger when the parents and child have warm relationships (e.g., Andrews et al., 1997), but similar moderating effects have yet to be consistently demonstrated when examining pathways between hostile interparental and child behaviors (Formosa, Gonzales, & Aiken, 2000).

The Cognitive-Contextual Framework

The cognitive-contextual framework, which is rooted in social-cognitive theories of interpersonal relations, is another established theory of interparental conflict (Grych & Cardoza-Fernandes, 2001; Grych & Fincham, 1990). A common assumption of the emotional security hypothesis and the cognitive-contextual framework is that the relationship between interparental conflict and child adjustment hinges on the specific ways the parents manage their conflicts and on the child subjective evaluations of the implications these conflicts have for child well-being. However, the cognitive-contextual framework differs from the emotional security hypothesis in placing heavier emphasis on understanding how the cognitive dimensions of the child's appraisals shape the impact of conflict on child adjustment (Grych & Fincham, 1993; Grych, Seid, & Fincham, 1992).

In the cognitive-contextual framework, two dimensions of appraisals play particularly pivotal roles in explaining why interparental conflict increases child vulnerability to maladjustment. First, exposure to high levels of parental conflict may pose a risk to child adjustment by heightening the child's perceptions of threat posed by conflicts. Perceived threat is specifically characterized by a child's analysis of how threatening the conflict is to his or her well-being and ability to successfully cope with the conflict. In the first part of an unfolding series of processes, a child who experiences angry, hostile, and unresolved disputes between his or her parents is posited to be more prone to perceive parents' conflicts as threatening than a child whose parents manage their conflicts in more constructive ways (e.g., mild anger, progress toward resolving differences). Perceptions of threat, in turn, are conceptualized as increasing the specific risk for child internalizing symptoms by increasing the proclivity to feelings of anxiety, dysphoria, and helplessness (Grych, Fincham, et al., 2000). Conversely, recent refinements of the cognitive-contextual framework suggest that processes other than perceived threat (e.g., modeling, parent-child relations, emotional reactivity) may be responsible for the elevated externalizing symptoms of children from high conflict homes (Grych, Fincham, et al., 2000).

Second, the child's attributions regarding the cause of conflict are also presumed to mediate the relationship between interparental conflict and child maladjustment. A primary assumption is that a child who is exposed to angry, hostile, and unresolved conflicts is likely to assume the role of parental peacekeeper, arbitrator, and confidante. However, the child's involvement in the conflict is not likely to play a significant role in resolving complex parental disputes or improving difficult interparental relations. Thus, as the child increasingly bears the formidable responsibility of preserving family and marital harmony, the child may be especially prone to believing that he or she is at least partly to blame for the continuing interparental disputes and difficulties. Perceived blame, in turn, is theorized to play a particularly significant role in the genesis of internalizing symptoms by increasing children's feelings of guilt, shame, poor self-worth, and helplessness.

The few studies that have examined the role of the child's perceived threat and self-blame in models of interparental conflict have provided some support for the proposed mediational pathways. Grych, Fincham, et al. (2000) reported that perceived threat and self-blame were consistent mediators of the relationship between interparental conflict and child internalizing symptoms for samples of children recruited from the community and battered women's shelters—the only exception being that perceived blame failed to mediate the risk posed by interparental conflict for girls in the shelter sample. Consistent with hypotheses, appraisals of conflict did not account for links between interparental conflict and externalizing symptoms. Findings from another recent study suggested that perceived threat and self-blame consistently mediated the link between parental conflict severity and boys' and girls' adjustment in the prediction of internalizing symptoms but not externalizing symptoms (Dadds, Atkinson, Turner, Blums, & Lendich, 1999; also see Kerig, 1998b). However, other studies have failed to find evidence for the mediational role of self-blame and perceived threat (Kerig, 1998a).

Indirect Effects Models

Several conceptual models have hypothesized that co-occurring disruptions in parenting and the parent-child relationship account, at least in part, for why interparental conflict is associated with child symptomatology. For example, in his seminal review of the literature, Emery (1982) described the role of parent-child relationship processes (i.e., attachment, parenting) as central to understanding the risk of parental conflict in two of his three primary explanations. Although explanations addressing the role of parent-child relations have been further developed, expanded, and differentiated over the past two decades, these indirect effects models share the same assumption that interparental conflict affects child functioning through its association with disruptions in the parent-child relationship.

The two classes of parent-child processes that have received the most conceptual attention are parenting practices and parent-child attachment relationships. Indirect effects models of parenting suggest that interparental conflict is associated with disruptions in one or more domains of parenting, including (a) poor behavioral control of the child reflected in lax monitoring and inconsistent or harsh discipline; (b) greater psychological control characterized by efforts to control the child through the manipulation and exploitation of the parent-child bond (e.g., love withdrawal, guilt induction, intrusiveness, criticism); and (c) lack of warmth, acceptance, and emotional availability. These parenting difficulties, in turn, are theorized to increase the child's risk for adjustment problems, including internalizing and externalizing symptoms (Crockenberg & Covey, 1991; Erel & Burman, 1995; Fauber & Long, 1991; Holden & Miller, 1999). Empirical support for these hypothesized pathways has been quite strong. Experimental studies and sequential analyses of natural interactions have shown that disruptions in parenting increase following interparental disputes (Christensen & Margolin, 1988; Jouriles & Farris, 1992; Mahoney, Boggio, & Jouriles, 1996). In addition, parental emotional unavailability, poor behavioral control, and psychological control have been shown to account for at least part of the association between interparental conflict and child adjustment (Erel, Margolin, & John, 1998; Fauber, Forehand, Thomas, & Wierson, 1990; Gonzalez et al., 2000; Harold et al., 1997; Webster-Stratton & Hammond, 1999).

Attachment theorists have hypothesized that interparental conflict is also linked with insecure parent-child attachments through at least two mechanisms. First, parenting difficulties characterized by a lack of warmth, sensitivity, and acceptance may accompany interparental conflict and account for its association with parent-child attachment insecurity. Consistent with this hypothesis, parental emotional unavailability (e.g., hostility, lack of support, sensitivity, or warmth) was identified as a partial mediator in the link between marital conflict and parent-child attachment insecurity (Frosch, Mangelsdorf, & McHale, 2000; Owen & Cox, 1997). Second, the frightening and frightened behaviors exhibited by parents during conflict may directly affect the child's attachment security by undermining the sense of confidence in parents as sources of support and protection (Owen & Cox, 1997; Main & Hesse, 1990). Supporting this hypothesis, studies have shown that the association between marital conflict and parent-child attachment insecurity remains robust even after statistically controlling for parental sensitivity and warmth (Frosch et al., 2000; Owen & Cox, 1997). As an evolving product of the effects of interparental conflict and parenting, the quality of the child's sense of security in parent-child attachment relationships has been associated with a wide range of developmental outcomes and problems (Colin, 1996).

Although a common hypothesis of indirect effects models is that parenting processes mediate the effects of interparental conflict, these models differ from each other in the strength they ascribe to the mediating effects. Weak models of indirect effects, which make fewer assumptions about the power of parenting processes as mediators, postulate that parenting is one of many mechanisms that may account for the relationship between interparental conflict and child functioning. Thus, parenting is presumed to be a partial, rather than a full, mediator of the risk posed by interparental conflict (Emery, Fincham, & Cummings, 1992; Gottman & Katz, 1989; Grych & Fincham, 1990; Webster-Stratton & Hammond, 1999). Consistent with this form of indirect effects, the emotional security hypothesis proposes that parenting is one of many processes that may account for the risk posed by interparental conflict.

Conversely, strong models of indirect effects assume that parenting processes are the primary or sole mediators of interparental conflict. That is, parenting processes are theorized to provide a complete explanation for why interparental conflict is related to child adjustment (Erel et al., 1998; Fauber et al., 1990; Fauber & Long, 1991; Patterson, DeBaryshe, & Ramsey, 1989). For example, Fauber and Long concluded that "it is at the site of parenting practices that conflict has its effect on children, and so it is at this level that the problem should be addressed" (p. 816). In conceptualizing parental conflict as a *contextual variable* in their model, Fauber and Long specifically argued that "most contextual variables ultimately have their impact on children through some disturbance in family process, and more specifically in disrupted parenting practices" (p. 816).

Research has not definitively addressed which type of indirect effects model provides a better representation of the data in predicting children's long-term outcomes. In support of the strong model, some studies have shown that parenting practices fully account for the association between parental conflict and child adjustment (Fauber et al., 1990; Mann & MacKenzie, 1996). However, these studies generally employ more rigorous and comprehensive assessments of parenting practices than parental conflict. Thus, these findings may be largely attributed to the discrepancies in the psychometric properties of measures of parenting and interparental conflict. Other studies have found support for the weak model of indirect effects. For example, Webster-Stratton and Hammond (1999) reported that interparental conflict continued to be associated with child conduct problems even after taking into account critical parenting and parental responsiveness. Likewise, carefully controlled, experimental manipulations of interadult conflict have shown that the introduction of destructive forms of conflict are associated with elevated levels of distress and aggression in children (Cummings & Davies, 1994). The handful of available longitudinal studies have also indicated that interparental discord is associated with subsequent psychological difficulties (e.g, Davies & Windle, 2001; Gottman & Katz, 1989; Katz & Gottman, 1997; Kline, Johnston, & Tschann, 1991; Wierson, Forehand, & McCombs, 1988). However, these lines of research have also been limited by the failure to simultaneously assess child experiences with parenting practices and child reactions to parental conflict within models of child psychological adjustment. More comprehensive tests of processes underlying parental conflict will require methodological designs that simultaneously measure both direct and indirect mechanisms with comparable levels of methodological rigor.

CONCEPTUAL AIMS AND SIGNIFICANCE OF THE STUDIES

Guided by the model in Figure 1, the set of four programmatic studies described in this *Monograph* share the goal of advancing an understanding of the role child emotional security plays in the link between interparental conflict and child maladjustment. To provide a conservative test of our model, the studies are designed to address four main research questions by utilizing diverse samples (Welsh and U.S. samples), measurement strategies (e.g., different informants), methodological designs (analogue-experimental, field designs), and analytic models (from more microscopic to macroscopic analyses). Although progress has been made in empirically identifying precise associations between exposure to forms of parental conflict, child responses, and their long-term adjustment, previous research has failed to identify hypotheses and design studies that permit tests of the relative efficacy of multiple theoretical explanations. Findings from previous studies often lend support for multiple conceptual models. For example, the emotional security hypothesis, social learning theory, and the cognitive-contextual framework share the common hypothesis that the child's negative appraisals, emotions, and behaviors in response to parental conflicts mediate the link between parental conflict and child psychological maladjustment. Thus, regardless of the specific theory or theories that served as a guide for existing studies, a common caveat of previous empirical studies is that multiple theories may "provide viable mechanisms that help account for links between marital discord and child adjustment" (Davies & Cummings, 1998, p. 135).

In building on earlier research, a next important step is to move to a new stage of research that identifies and tests focal hypotheses that discriminate among the different theories of interparental conflict. Toward this goal, we test hypotheses derived from the emotional security hypothesis in the context of corresponding predictions made by other theories. Brief descriptions of the significance of each of the four themes and how the studies are designed to test the research questions are provided in the following sections.

How Does the Child Respond to Destructive Forms of Parental Conflict?

Beginning at a microscopic level of analysis, the first study, described in Chapter II, explores the first link in the mediational chain (Path 1 in Figure 1). The specific aim of this study is to examine the nature of the relationship between destructive forms of parental conflict and child responding to conflict from the child's perspective of preserving a sense of security. Previous research has shown that children are especially likely to exhibit negative emotions and behaviors when adult or parental conflicts are characterized by unresolved hostility, personal threats, violence, and child-related disagreements (Cummings, Vogel, Cummings, & El-Sheikh, 1989; Davies et al., 1999; El-Sheikh, Cummings, & Reiter, 1996; Grych & Fincham, 1993; Laumakis, Margolin, & John, 1998). However, this general pattern of findings supports multiple conceptual models, including the emotional security hypothesis, the cognitive-contextual framework, and the social learning theory (Davies et al., 1999).

To address this issue, Study 1 is designed to advance the study of the relationship between destructive forms of parental conflict and child functioning by identifying and testing hypotheses that distinguish the emotional security hypothesis from social learning theory. Each theory makes predictions about the relationship between specific conflict tactics and the child's specific emotional and behavioral responses at a micro-analytic level. Processes of imitation and modeling in social learning theory lead to predictions that are fundamentally different than those in the emotional security hypothesis.

Testing these different predictions poses some methodological challenges. For example, in daily, naturalistic contexts, it is very difficult, if not impossible, to test these predictions because it is impossible to adequately define and identify the relationship between specific forms of conflict and child responding. To maximize precision, control, and statistical power, this study utilizes an analogue design in which the child witnesses several well-defined videotaped clips depicting parameters of adult conflict that are pertinent to testing the different hypotheses of the two theories.

Does Emotional Security Prospectively Account for the Link Between Parental Conflict and Child Adjustment?

Expanding the scope of inquiry beyond the link between conflict and emotional security, the second study, described in Chapter III, is designed to test a key proposition of the emotional security hypothesis: Child emotional security in the context of interparental conflict accounts for the link between parental conflict and child adjustment problems. Thus, in the context of Figure 1, the second study is designed to address (a) links between interparental conflict and child emotional insecurity (Path 1), (b) interrelations among the three component processes (Path 3), and (c) associations between emotional insecurity and child maladjustment (Path 4). Previous empirical support for the mediational role of child security is largely based on incomplete tests that are limited to (a) relations between marital conflict and child emotional security processes, (b) emotional security processes and child outcomes, or (c) mediational tests involving a narrow subset of the indicators of emotional security (e.g., a few indicators of internal representations).

In the only published study to assess the role of the three component processes of security in models of parental conflict and child adjustment, Davies and Cummings (1998) reported that the child's emotional reactivity and internal representations of parental conflict accounted, in part, for the link between parental conflict and child maladjustment. Although this exploratory study provided some promising insights into the operation of emotional security, it also suffered from several limitations. Reliance on a small sample of U.S. children and families and single analogue assessments of emotional security limited the statistical power of the analyses and the generalizability of the findings. To overcome these limitations, Study 2 in this *Monograph* utilizes more powerful statistical tests (i.e., structural equation models) with a larger sample of Welsh children and families. Another important step is to examine whether emotional security remains a robust explanatory mechanism using diverse measurement batteries and methodological designs. For example, rather than assessing indicators of insecurity in single analogue simulations of conflict, this study examines indicators of child insecurity through children's reports of their responses to naturalistic parental conflicts. In addition, this study extends the concurrent nature of earlier tests of the emotional security hypothesis by employing a prospective examination of relationships between interparental conflict, child emotional security, and child adjustment.

Evaluating the emotional security hypothesis as a heuristic for research hinges on demonstrating that it maintains its explanatory power in relation to alternative theories on the role of child characteristics as mediators of parental conflict. In this regard, the cognitive-contextual framework is a prominent theory that addresses the mediating role of the child's social-cognitive processes in the link between interparental conflict and child adjustment. Therefore, the second study is designed to take the literature a step further by simultaneously examining emotional security and social-cognitive appraisals of perceived threat and self-blame as mediators in the association between parental conflict and child psychological symptoms. Integrating these two theories into a single analytic model raises critical questions for the second generation of research. For example, does emotional security continue to account for the link between parental conflict and child maladjustment even after taking into account social-cognitive processes such as self-blame and perceived threat? Do perceived threat and self-blame help account for associations between interparental conflict and child internalizing and externalizing symptoms?

Does Emotional Security Account for the Effects of Parental Conflict in the Broader Family Context?

In broadening the scope of inquiry still further, the third study, described in Chapter IV, advances a family-wide model of child emotional security by embedding the study of mediational pathways among parental conflict, emotional security, and child adjustment in the larger context of parenting and parent-child relations. Research testing indirect effects models has underscored that family processes such as parenting practices and

23

parent-child relations constitute significant pathways mediating the links between interparental conflict and child adjustment. In support of these models, parental lack of warmth, poor behavioral control (e.g., lax monitoring), and psychological control (e.g., guilt induction, love withdrawal, discounting feelings) have been shown to account, in part, for the association between interparental conflict and child maladjustment (Fauber et al., 1990; Mann & MacKenzie, 1996). However, because empirical tests have rarely examined direct and indirect effects models in the same study, integrating the study of direct and indirect pathways into a single, unifying model of emotional security is an important undertaking. Consistent with the overarching theme of this *Monograph*, this integration also permits tests of the relative efficacy of the emotional security hypothesis in the context of complementary explanations derived from indirect effects models and attachment theory.

Toward this goal, the third study constitutes the first, exploratory foray into testing whether the joint influence of destructive parental conflict and poor parenting practices increases child vulnerability to psychological symptomatology by undermining the child's ability to preserve emotional security in the interparental and parent-child relationships. Integrating direct and indirect models into a single model generates a wealth of new questions. First, do the mediational pathways between interparental conflict, child security in the context of interparental conflict, and child maladjustment remain robust (Paths 1 and 4 in Figure 1) over and above the indirect effects of parenting practices and parent-child attachment security? Or, as strong versions of indirect effects models would propose, do parenting practices and parent-child attachment security fully account for link between interparental conflict and child adjustment? Second, are the indirect effects of parenting in associations between parental conflict and child adjustment ultimately accounted for by insecurity in the parent-child relationship (Path 5 in Figure 1)? Third, is children's insecurity in a specific family relationship (e.g., interparental, parent-child) primarily related to their experiential histories within that particular relationship or their experiences in multiple family relationships (Paths 1 and 5 in Figure 1)? Finally, are forms of insecurity across different family relationships (i.e., insecurity in the context of interparental conflict, attachment insecurity) associated with similar or different forms of psychological maladjustment (Paths 4 and 5 in Figure 1)?

Do Family Characteristics Potentiate or Buffer the Child From the Risk Posed by Parental Conflict?

Although the emotional security framework has cast family characteristics as potentiating or protective factors in mediational pathways between parental conflict, emotional insecurity, and child adjustment (e.g., Cummings & Davies, 1995; Davies & Cummings, 1994), research has yet to systematically identify the specific family characteristics that act as moderators. To gain a further understanding of the interplay between interparental conflict and other family characteristics, the fourth study, described in Chapter V, examines the moderating role of family contextual characteristics in these mediational pathways. Guided by our earlier conceptual model, family contextual characteristics are specifically hypothesized to play moderating roles in associations between (a) parental conflict and child emotional insecurity in the context of interparental conflict (Path 6 in Figure 1), and (b) child emotional insecurity and psychological problems (Path 7 in Figure 1). Because social learning theory provides an alternative hypothesis about the nature of the moderating effects of family contextual variables, we test the hypotheses derived from both theories to examine the relative utility of each in explaining the pattern of results.

In addressing Path 6, children from families that evidence high levels of instability (e.g., dissolution, turnover of caregivers) or relational distress (e.g., parent-child relationship difficulties) have more at stake in monitoring and repairing any damaged relationships in an already fragile family system. The resulting preoccupation and vigilance with interparental relations are especially likely to undermine child insecurity when the child is exposed to high levels of parental conflict. Thus, we specifically hypothesize that family instability and relationship difficulties may potentiate the association between parental conflict on child insecurity. By the same token, bouts of parental conflict that occur in a warm, cohesive family environment may signify that any adverse effects caused by conflict are short-lived and well-managed by the parents. Thus, parental conflict may not substantially undermine child security when it occurs in the context of cohesive family relations. Likewise, anger expressed in parental conflict may simply reflect a larger tendency for parents to express both positive and negative emotion (i.e., marital expressiveness), a pattern that has been associated with social competence in children (Cassidy, Parke, Butkovsky, & Braungart, 1992). Expressions of negative and positive affect may elicit family discussions and explanations about the nature, causes, and constructive consequences of emotion that, in turn, have been linked with subsequent increases in socioemotional understanding (Dunn, Brown, & Beardsall, 1991). High rates of positive affect or support in the context of anger and conflict may also reduce child emotional insecurity, thereby freeing the child to better understand how people manage and resolve disputes. Thus, family cohesiveness and parental expressiveness may act as protective factors that help to offset the risk posed by parental conflict to the child's sense of security.

Family contextual variables may also be associated with the weakening or amplification of the links between child emotional security and psychological problems (see Path 7 in Figure 1). Guided by our earlier theoretical model, insecure children are hypothesized to be especially vulnerable to psychological problems when they also have to deal with other sources of adversity in the family, such as parenting disturbances and histories of family instability. These indicators of emotional and relational vulnerability in the larger family context may specifically serve to broaden and deepen the child's worries, anxieties, and insecurities and, in the process, set the stage for more pervasive internalizing symptoms. By the same token, the child is theorized to be less likely to manifest psychological problems when emotional insecurity is embedded in a broader context of supportive and harmonious family relations (i.e., interparental relationship satisfaction, family cohesion). More specifically, concerns about security in the interparental relationship may be less prominent in the life of the child who has the benefit of gaining support, confidence, and skills necessary to cope with other important challenges. Consequently, it is hypothesized that supportive family relations will protect the child who exhibits high levels of insecurity from developing psychological problems.

In contrast to the emotional security hypothesis, social learning theory suggests that certain family contextual factors reflecting warm, cohesive family relationships may actually potentiate, rather than dilute the relationship between interparental conflict and child negative reactions to conflict. Rooted in the assumption that children are more likely to model the behaviors of adults they admire, trust, and love, social learning theory actually hypothesizes that the relationship between aggressive conflict tactics between parents and children's aggressive behaviors would be especially pronounced for children who have cohesive, trusting, warm relationships with their parents.

II. STUDY 1: CHILD RESPONSES TO INTERPARENTAL CONFLICT: COMPARING THE RELATIVE ROLES OF EMOTIONAL SECURITY AND SOCIAL LEARNING PROCESSES

The question of theoretical interest in this study is whether the pattern of associations between specific conflict tactics and child responses support predictions derived from the emotional security hypothesis, social learning theory, or both. Empirical advances in process models of interparental conflict have been limited by the tendency to utilize the emotional security hypothesis and social learning theory as post hoc explanations for findings. Furthermore, when a priori tests of theoretical predictions have been conducted, researchers have typically tested hypotheses from the two theories in isolation from each other. As a result, studies have failed to distinguish between hypotheses of emotional security and social learning theories (e.g., Davies & Cummings, 1998; Davies et al., 1999). However, our conceptual update and review provides a basis for articulating four primary differences across the theories in the hypotheses made about the nature of associations between conflict tactics and the child's responses to conflict.

First, each theory makes different predictions about child reactions to specific forms of conflict. Although emotional security and social learning theories hold that children should evidence distress in response to angry or aggressive adults, the emotional security hypothesis specifically predicts that children will be more negatively affected when the topics of the arguments have implications for their own sense of security. Child-related themes and threats to the intactness of the family are especially likely to undermine the child's sense of security because they signify the possibility of family dissolution and potential spillover of hostility from interparental conflicts to parent-child interactions (Davies & Cummings, 1994; Laumakis et al., 1998). Thus, the emotional security hypothesis specifically predicts that the child will experience more distress when topics of conflict center on the child as opposed to the adults, or convey threats

27

to the stability of the family as opposed to other more general expressions of verbal hostility. By comparison, social learning theory does not make distinctions between these forms of conflict in understanding variations in child responding. Rather, emphasis on modeling processes in social learning theory leads to the prediction that child negative emotional reactions are more pronounced when the conflict is characterized by physical aggression than by verbal expressions of threats to the family. In contrast, because physical aggression and verbal threats to family stability are each salient threats to the child's emotional security, the emotional security hypothesis does not make any specific predictions about differences in distress across these conflict tactics (Cummings, 1998).

The second primary difference across the theories concerns their predictions about the prevalence of behavioral responses in the face of destructive parental conflicts. Social learning theory postulates that the child imitates the aggressive behaviors and generalized scripts for aggression when exposed to parental disputes characterized by aggression and hostility. Thus, aggressive reactions in the form of gestures, behaviors, or verbalizations are expected to be particularly common responses to angry, hostile disputes by parents (Bandura, 1973). In contrast, the emotional security hypothesis emphasizes that exposure to destructive conflict motivates the child to regulate exposure to parental conflict through attempts to intervene or avoid the conflict (Cummings & Davies, 1996; Davies & Cummings, 1994). Aggressive forms of intervening in conflicts may sometimes reflect forms of regulating exposure to conflict, but they are not necessarily expected to resemble adults' angry or aggressive acts and only constitute a subset of methods for intervening in the conflict. Accordingly, whereas social learning theory hypothesizes that child hostility and aggression are the predominant responses to intense conflicts, the emotional security hypothesis predicts that intervention and avoidance are the most commonly endorsed responses to destructive conflict (Davies et al., 2002).

Third, differential predictions regarding emotional reactions provide another basis for distinguishing the two theories. Although the emotional security hypothesis suggests that the child responds with general distress (e.g., fear, sadness, anger) in the face of destructive forms of conflict, the current articulation of the theory results in the prediction that fear is a particularly powerful index of insecurity (see Chapter I). Thus, the more precise hypothesis is that fearful responding would be more likely to increase than other forms of negative affect as the child is exposed to increasingly destructive conflicts (i.e., physical violence rather than verbal hostility). In contrast, within social learning theory the salience of aggressive models increases from exposure to verbally aggressive models to physically aggressive models. By extension, social learning theory predicts that the child is more likely to experience anger and hostility when exposed to physical conflict than to verbal conflict.

Fourth, the two theories vary in their conceptualizations of the role of gender in parental conflict. The emotional security hypothesis makes no specific predictions about whether the child is more affected by the conflict behaviors of the same-sex or opposite-sex parent (Crockenberg & Langrock, 2001a; Snyder, 1998). However, explanations influenced by social learning theory predict that same-sex parents are more salient as aggressive models than opposite-sex parents (Bandura, 1973; Crockenberg & Langrock, 2001a). It follows that boys are more likely to imitate the aggressive behaviors of fathers than of mothers, whereas the girls are more likely to imitate the aggressive behavior of mothers than of fathers.

Testing these four sets of hypotheses poses significant methodological challenges because the predictions require a focus on very precise dimensions of family and child functioning, including specific conflict tactics (e.g., child-rearing, physical aggression), particular types of child emotions and behaviors, and specific characteristics of the adult combatants (i.e., gender). Field designs that rely on assessments of family process in naturalistic contexts do not have the precision or control necessary to adequately test these hypotheses. Illustrating the difficulties with precision, assessments of family functioning in everyday contexts often fail to adequately distinguish between important conflict tactics (e.g., threats to family stability versus verbal aggression) and to capture relatively infrequent, but conceptually significant, forms of conflict (e.g., physical aggression). Likewise, the relatively low levels of control in field designs also make it difficult to disentangle the effects of specific conflict tactics from the larger constellation of covarying family and contextual factors that may also influence the child's responses. Given the significance of maximizing precision and control in tests of these hypotheses, we utilize an analogue design in which presentations of well-defined, conflict stimuli are carefully controlled. The child is specifically introduced to conflict scenarios between adults by means of specific videotaped clips in a laboratory setting.

METHODS

Participants

The participants included 327 sixth-grade children (159 boys, 168 girls) recruited from seven schools in Wales (M age = 11.7 years; range 11–12 years). Participants were part of a larger, longitudinal study of Welsh children and families. Approximately 98% of the sample originated in Great Britain, with the remaining being of primarily Indian or Sri Lankan origin.

The mean age for mothers was 41 years (range 29–55 years); the mean age for fathers was 44 years (range 30–64). Thirty-six percent of mothers had completed secondary education only, 34% had completed technical or vocational training, and 29% had graduated university or beyond; 32% of fathers had completed secondary education only, 30% had completed technical or vocational training, and 38% had graduated from a university. The majority of children lived with both biological parents (87%); small proportions of children lived with biological mothers and stepfathers (12%) or biological fathers and stepmothers (1%).

Procedure

Videotaped analogue. Children participated in an analogue video procedure conducted in a group setting in a school classroom. Children were shown videos (30 seconds to 1 minute in length) of a Welsh man and woman interacting. To more fully engage the participants in the task, the actors in the videotapes were carefully selected to reflect the typical ages and dialect of the children's parents. The modes of conflict expression considered in this study were randomly ordered and included the following: (a) physical aggression toward the spouse (increasingly angry verbalizations and gestures culminates in one parent forcefully pushing the other); (b) physical aggression toward inanimate objects (increasingly angry verbalizations and gestures culminates in one parent throwing a household object); (c) threat to the intactness of the family (initial frustration escalates as one parent states angrily that the other's behavior is typical, threatens to leave, then leaves); (d) verbal hostility (initial frustration escalates to angry tones of voice and verbalizations); and (e) nonverbal hostility (after a short bout of questioning about the issue, one parent expresses dissatisfaction and anger through gestures such as crossed arms and frowning).

Each mode of conflict expression was presented to the children twice, once with the conflict centered on a child-related theme (helping the child with homework) and once with the conflict centered on an adult-related theme (choosing a television program). Affect level, specific behaviors, and degree of resolution were consistent across the two scenarios. Order of presentation was counterbalanced, with 202 children viewing the conflict involving the adult-related theme first and 125 viewing the child-theme conflict first. The initiating parent in the conflict was a between-subjects factor and was counterbalanced across children (206 children saw dad as initiator and 121 saw mom as initiator). Before watching each video, the child was asked to imagine that the actors were "mum" (mom) and dad. Following each scene, the child answered a series of questions on paper.

Interview questions and scoring. At the end of each segment, children answered two questions that described their responses as if they were in the same room with their mum and dad during the disagreement. First, to assess their emotional reactivity, the child was asked "How would you feel?" and was given the option to answer *happy, angry, sad, scared,* or *okay.* The child was then asked "How much would you feel that way?" and indicated the degree of emotion on a 5-point scale from *very little* to *a whole lot;* 0 was assigned to any emotion not endorsed by the child. Second, to assess endorsements of behavior, the child was presented with the free response question, "What would you have done if you had been in the same room as them?" A research assistant blind to the hypotheses of the study coded the child's self-reported behavioral responses to the conflict scenes for the presence or absence of (a) two forms of regulation of conflict exposure central to the emotional security hypothesis: intervention and avoidance, and (b) four forms of hostility central to social learning theory: physical aggression toward a person, physical aggression toward an object, verbal hostility, and nonverbal hostility. Inter-rater reliability was established by having two coders independently rate 30 children.

Intervention was coded if the child endorsed any nonhostile strategy for intervening in the conflict (e.g., making suggestions for ways to solve the problem, asking or telling parents to work it out, comforting parents). Although hostile ways of intervening are considered to be reflections of insecurity in the emotional security hypothesis (e.g., yelling at parents to stop), they were not coded as intervention strategies, both to reduce conceptual overlap with the hostility constructs in social learning theory and to err on the side of providing a conservative estimate of the prevalence of intervention responses based on the emotional security hypothesis. *Avoidance* was coded if the child endorsed an attempt to create physical or emotional distance from parents' conflicts (e.g., leaving the room or house, pretending not to hear the conflict). Kappas, indexing inter-rater reliability, were .90 for intervention and .89 for avoidance. Intervention and avoidance were considered as discrete constructs in some analyses, but were combined for other analyses to form an overall *regulation* of conflict exposure variable indexing the presence of either intervention or avoidance.

The remaining four codes reflect behaviors of central interest to social learning theory. *Physical aggression toward a person* was coded if the child endorsed any act of physical aggression toward any individual (e.g., hitting, slapping, hurting someone), whereas *physical aggression toward an inanimate object* was coded if the child endorsed any act of physical aggression toward or with an object (e.g., slamming doors, or throwing, breaking, or hitting something). *Verbal hostility* was coded if the child endorsed any

31

outward expression of hostility with words (e.g., arguments with parents, yelling, sarcasm, insults), and *nonverbal hostility* was coded if the child endorsed any outward expression of hostility that did not involve words (e.g., sulking, slamming doors, storming out of the room, scoffing). Codes were not mutually exclusive. Thus, nonverbal hostility was coded if the child reported physical aggression. Kappa coefficients, indexing inter-rater reliability for the hostility codes, were all above .81 for each of the four codes in each focal conflict scene (range: .82 to .99).

For some analyses, measures of hostile behavior were designed to assess *imitation,* which was defined as the endorsement of a specific type of hostile behavior (e.g., verbal hostility) that corresponded to the tactics of hostility expressed by the parents in the simulated conflicts (e.g., verbal hostility). The four hostility codes also were combined to generate a code indexing the presence of behavioral *dysregulation* in response to each interparental conflict scene (i.e., *any* nomination of physical aggression toward a person, physical aggression toward an object, verbal hostility, or nonverbal hostility regardless of parents' specific conflict tactics).

RESULTS

To test the four main hypotheses, a priori tests were conducted for children's responses to the five destructive marital conflict tactics: physical aggression toward the spouse, physical aggression toward an object, threat to intactness of the family, verbal hostility, nonverbal hostility. *Child gender* was included in all analyses and *parent gender* was considered when it was hypothesized to be a theoretically meaningful factor.

Child Responses to Different Forms of Interparental Conflict

The emotional security hypothesis proposes that a child experiences greater distress in response to conflict in which the topic is characterized as child-related as opposed to adult-related, and threatening to the intactness of the family rather than simply reflecting general verbal hostility. A series of analyses of variance (ANOVAs), which employed a multivariate approach to repeated measures, were conducted to compare child negative emotional responses (i.e., sum of *mad, sad, scared*) to arguments about child-related and adult-related topics for each of the five types of conflicts (i.e., threat to intactness, physical aggression toward spouse, physical aggression toward object, verbal hostility, nonverbal hostility). Children responded with greater negativity to child-related than to adult-related topics for conflicts characterized by (a) threat to intactness (M = 2.88, SD = 1.15, and M = 2.54, SD = 1.34, respectively), $F(1, 325)$ = 19.37, $p < .001$, η^2 = .06; (b) physical aggression toward the spouse (M = 2.82, SD = 1.20, and M = 2.32, SD = 1.24, respectively), $F(1, 325)$ = 43.35, $p < .001$, η^2 = .12; and (c) verbal hostility (M = 1.97, SD = 1.28, and M = 1.05, SD = 1.22, respectively), $F(1, 325)$ = 111.28, $p < .001$, η^2 = .26.

Significant Child Gender × Conflict Topic interactions were found for child negative emotional responding to physical aggression toward an object, $F(1, 325)$ = 6.79, p = .01, η^2 = .02, and to nonverbal hostility, $F(1, 325)$ = 4.37, $p < .05$, η^2 = .01. Simple effects tests revealed that boys reported more negativity in response to child-related themes than to adult-related themes for both physical aggression toward an object (M = 2.55, SD =1.16, and M = 2.06, SD = 1.22, respectively), $F(1, 325)$ = 23.06, $p < .001$, η^2 = .07, and nonverbal hostility (M = 1.80, SD = 1.45, and M = 1.28, SD = 1.24, respectively), $F(1, 325)$ = 18.55, $p < .001$, η^2 = .05. Differences in girls' negativity in response to child-related and adult-related conflicts were in the hypothesized direction but were not statistically significant for either physical aggression toward an object (M = 2.58, SD = 1.15, and M = 2.46, SD = 1.08, respectively), $F(1, 325)$ = 1.43, p = .23, η^2 = .00, or nonverbal hostility (M = 1.53, SD = 1.32, and M = 1.36, SD = 1.20, respectively), $F(1, 325)$ = 2.05, p = .15, η^2 = .01.

An ANOVA that employed a multivariate approach to repeated measures was also conducted to examine whether children reacted more negatively to verbal threats to the intactness of the family than to general verbal hostility. A significant main effect for conflict topic, $F(1, 325)$ = 367.69, $p < .001$, = η^2 = .53, indicated that children reacted more negatively to threats to intactness (M = 2.71, SD = 1.04) than they did to verbal hostility (M = 1.51, SD = 0.97).

In contrast, social learning theory hypothesizes that children's negative emotionality will be especially likely to increase when the children are exposed to conflicts in which adults are providing more salient models of aggression (i.e., physical aggression toward the spouse > verbal threats to intactness). A repeated measures ANOVA was again conducted to compare child negative emotional responses to threat to intactness and physical aggression toward the spouse. A significant Child Gender × Conflict interaction emerged, $F(1, 325)$ = 5.49, $p < .05$, η^2 = .02. Simple effects tests revealed that girls did not differ in their negative emotional responses to conflict characterized by threat to intactness (M = 2.69, SD = 1.06) and physical aggression toward the spouse (M = 2.70, SD = 0.95). However, counter to social learning hypotheses, boys reported more negativity in response to threat to intactness (M = 2.73, SD = 1.03) than to physical aggression toward the spouse, (M = 2.44, SD = 1.07), $F(1,325)$ = 10.07, $p < .005$, η^2 = .03.

Child Endorsements of Behavioral Responses to Parental Conflict

The emotional security hypothesis predicts that a child's efforts to regulate exposure to conflict through intervention or avoidance are primary behavioral responses toward maintaining emotional security in response to interparental conflict. In contrast, social learning theory hypothesizes that the child's hostile and aggressive responses are primary behavioral responses stemming from emulating the hostile adult behaviors occurring in parental conflicts.

The relative prevalence of specific regulatory behaviors and specific imitative behaviors. As a first test of these hypotheses, repeated measures ANOVAs were conducted to compare the relative rates of intervention and avoidance with rates of specific imitation behaviors in response to the four interparental conflict tactics (physical aggression toward spouse, physical aggression toward object, verbal hostility, nonverbal hostility). Imitation was defined by the child's endorsement of a specific hostile behavior (i.e., physical aggression toward a person, physical aggression toward an object, verbal hostility, nonverbal hostility, respectively) that emulated the specific conflict tactics used in the conflict vignettes. Means and standard deviations of the behavioral responses are reported in Table 1. The child was presented with each conflict tactic twice, with responding scored 0 or 1.

TABLE 1

MEANS AND STANDARD DEVIATIONS OF CHILD ENDORSEMENTS OF BEHAVIORAL
RESPONDING TO INTERPARENTAL CONFLICT TACTICS

	Interparental Conflict Tactic							
	Physical Aggression Toward Spouse		Physical Aggression Toward Object		Verbal Hostility		Nonverbal Hostility	
Child Behavior	M	SD	M	SD	M	SD	M	SD
Specific responses								
Intervention	0.38	0.39	0.41	0.40	0.53	0.38	0.42	0.38
Avoidance	0.30	0.38	0.31	0.39	0.17	0.28	0.18	0.29
Imitation	0.07	0.20	0.02	0.12	0.06	0.17	0.04	0.14
General responses								
Regulation	0.65	0.39	0.71	0.37	0.69	0.34	0.59	0.38
Dysregulation	0.18	0.30	0.11	0.24	0.11	0.22	0.10	0.22

Note.—Imitation is defined as the frequency of endorsement of (a) physical aggression toward a person for conflict vignettes involving physical aggression toward the spouse, (b) physical aggression toward an inanimate object for conflict vignettes involving physical aggression toward an object, (c) verbal hostility for conflict vignettes involving verbal hostility, and (d) nonverbal hostility for confict vignettes involving nonverbal hostility.

Thus, a mean of 0 would indicate a response did not occur, 0.5 that a response on average occurred one of the times, and a 1.0 that a response on average occurred both times.

The first set of ANOVAs compared children's endorsement of intervention behaviors and imitation behaviors. Children specifically endorsed more intervention than imitation behaviors for (a) physical aggression toward spouse, $F(1, 325) = 152.42$, $p < .001$, $\eta^2 = .32$; (b) physical aggression toward object, $F(1, 325) = 283.09$, $p < .001$, $\eta^2 = .47$; (c) verbal hostility, $F(1, 325) = 346.33$, $p < .001$, $\eta^2 = .52$; and (d) nonverbal hostility, $F(1, 325) = 259.91$, $p < .001$, $\eta^2 = .44$. Child gender was not a significant factor in any analyses. Another set of ANOVAs compared the relative rates of avoidance behaviors and imitation behaviors. The results indicated that children endorsed more avoidance than imitation for (a) physical aggression toward spouse, $F(1, 325) = 84.50$, $p < .001$, $\eta^2 = .21$; (b) physical aggression toward object, $F(1, 325) = 165.72$, $p < .001$, $\eta^2 = .34$; (c) verbal hostility, $F(1, 325) = 36.36$, $p < .001$, $\eta^2 = .10$; and (d) nonverbal hostility, $F(1, 325) = 58.42$, $p < .001$, $\eta^2 = .15$. Child gender was not a significant factor in any analysis.

The relative prevalence of general regulatory behaviors and general behavioral dysregulation. In relaxing certain assumptions about strict imitation of specific behaviors, some social learning theorists have hypothesized that children will experience more general forms of behavioral dysregulation when they witness interparental hostility (Davis, Hops, Alpert, & Sheeber, 1998). Thus, examining the prevalence of specific imitative behaviors may provide an overly conservative test of modeling hypotheses in some versions of social learning theory. To address this possibility, another series of repeated measures ANOVAs were conducted to compare the relative rates of general regulation of exposure to conflict (i.e., any intervention or avoidance) and general behavioral dysregulation (i.e., any hostile or aggressive response) to the four forms of destructive parental conflict (see Table 1 for means and standard deviations). The results indicated that children endorsed more general regulation of conflict exposure than behavioral dysregulation for each of the conflicts, including, physical aggression toward spouse, $F(1, 325) = 202.32$, $p < .001$, $\eta^2 = .38$; physical aggression toward object, $F(1, 325) = 438.54$, $p < .001$, $\eta^2 = .57$; verbal hostility, $F(1, 325) = 465.44$, $p < .001$, $\eta^2 = .59$; and nonverbal hostility, $F(1, 325) = 341.61$, $p < .001$, $\eta^2 = .51$.

Child Specific Emotional Responses to Parental Conflict

The emotional security hypothesis predicts that increases in a child's fearful responding are especially likely to occur with exposure to increasingly destructive parental conflict. Conversely, social learning theory predicts that a child's angry responding progressively increases with exposure to more aggressive conflict tactics. Both theories share the hypothesis that conflict characterized by physical aggression toward the spouse is more destructive and angry than conflict containing only verbal hostility. Therefore, we selected these two conflict scenes for analyses of hypotheses for purposes of simultaneously evaluating the validity of the predictions derived from each theory. A repeated measures ANOVA was conducted to compare the intensity of fearful and angry responses to physical aggression toward the spouse and verbal hostility, respectively. A significant Emotion × Conflict interaction emerged, $F(1, 325) = 63.62$, $p < .001$, $\eta^2 = .16$. Simple effects tests indicated that children reported greater fear in response to physical aggression toward the spouse ($M = 1.37$, $SD = 1.25$) than in response to verbal hostility ($M = 0.18$, $SD = 0.45$), $F(1, 325) = 310.75$, $p < .001$, $\eta^2 = .49$. However, children's anger responses were not significantly different across verbally ($M = 0.89$, $SD = 0.96$) and physically aggressive ($M = 1.01$, $SD = 1.30$) conflicts, $F(1, 325) = 2.22$, $p = .14$, $\eta^2 = .01$. Simple effects tests of emotion further revealed that children responded with more anger than fear in response to parents' verbal hostility, $F(1, 325) = 120.21$, $p < .001$, $\eta^2 = .27$, but with more fear than anger in response to parents' physical aggression toward the spouse, $F(1, 325) = 7.57$, $p < .01$, $\eta^2 = .02$.

As a further test of these hypotheses, we also examined the relative frequency of each form of emotion as a function of interparental aggressiveness. The Wilcoxon signed rank test was conducted to compare the distributions of emotional responses to physical aggression and verbal hostility. One hundred thirteen children reported more anger in response to physical aggression than to verbal hostility (mean rank = 127.93), 117 children reported more anger in response to verbal hostility than to physical aggression toward the spouse (mean rank = 103.50), and 97 children reported equivalent levels of anger in response to the two conflict tactics. Consistent with ANOVA findings, anger did not increase as a function of marital aggression, $Z = -1.17$, $p = .243$. Conversely, 213 children reported more fear in response to physical aggression toward the spouse than to verbal hostility (mean rank = 115.53), 11 children reported more fear in response to verbal hostility than to physical aggression toward the spouse (mean rank = 53.86), and 103 children reported equivalent levels of fear in response to physical aggression toward the spouse and verbal hostility. The findings indicated that fear increased as a function of interparental aggressiveness, $Z = -12.41$, $p < .001$. Thus, across both types of analyses, exposure to increasing aggressiveness in conflict was associated with corresponding increases in fear but not anger.

Child Responses to Conflict Initiated by the Mother and Father

Although the emotional security hypothesis makes no definitive predictions about the role of parent and child gender in child responses to conflict, social learning theory hypothesizes that the child's responses vary as a function of the interaction between child and parent gender. Girls are specifically hypothesized to react with greater hostility to maternal expressions of aggression than to paternal displays of aggression, while boys are predicted to respond with greater hostility to fathers' rather than to mothers' aggression. A series of 2×2 (Parent Gender × Child Gender) ANOVAs were conducted to examine whether children's anger responses to each of the eight conflict scenes (physical aggression toward the spouse, physical aggression toward an object, verbal hostility, nonverbal hostility) varied as a function of parent and child gender. The only Child Gender × Parent Gender interaction that emerged was in response to physical aggression toward the spouse, $F(1, 323) = 3.86$, $p = .05$, $\eta^2 = .01$. However, simple effects tests revealed no significant differences in the means of boys' or girls' anger in response to fathers' and mothers' physical aggression. Thus, the results failed to support the hypothesis that children are more prone to model the same-gender parents' angry emotion during verbal, nonverbal, or physical hostility.

A series of 2×2 (Parent Gender × Child Gender) ANOVAs were also conducted to examine whether children's aggressive behavioral responses (i.e., imitation and general dysregulation) to each of the conflict scenes varied as a function of parent and child gender. The only significant Child Gender × Parent Gender interaction that emerged was for children's physical aggression toward an object in response to parents' physical aggression toward an object, $F(1, 323) = 6.55$, $p = .01$, $\eta^2 = .02$. Consistent with social learning theory hypotheses, simple effects tests indicated that girls reported more physical aggression toward an object in response to mothers' ($M = 0.05$, $SD = 0.17$) than to fathers' physical aggression toward an object ($M = 0.01$, $SD = 0.05$), $F(1, 323) = 5.44$, $p < .05$, $\eta^2 = .02$. However, contrary to predictions, boys' aggression object did not differ significantly as a function of parent gender ($M = 0.01$, $SD = 0.05$ for mother aggression; $M = 0.03$, $SD = 0.15$ for father aggression), $F(1, 323) = 1.70$, $p = .19$, $\eta^2 = .01$. Thus, no evidence emerged to indicate that boys model their fathers' behavior to a greater degree than they model their mothers' behavior, and only marginal support emerged for girls' modeling of aggression (1 significant effect out of 8 possible).

DISCUSSION

Children's reactions to exposure to marital conflict more closely fit the predictions of the emotional security hypothesis than the modeling

37

hypotheses. Children were more negatively reactive to *themes* of marital conflict posing elevated threats to child emotional security (i.e., child-related conflicts, threats to intactness of the family) than to otherwise equivalent conflict not involving such themes, whereas elevated aggressive modeling (i.e., physical aggression) was not more disturbing than some forms of less aggressive modeling that carried enhanced threat to emotional security (i.e., threats to intactness of the family). Consistent with the emotional security hypothesis, reports of *behavioral responses* were far more often consistent with children's concerns about regulating exposure to marital conflict (e.g., intervention, avoidance) than with notions of modeling adult aggressive behaviors in social learning theory. The pattern of children's *specific emotional responses* more consistently reflected predictions made by the emotional security than the modeling hypotheses. In support of the emotional security hypothesis, increases in interparental hostility were associated with increases in fearful responding in children. By contrast, the findings failed to support the social learning prediction that exposure to greater interparental hostility is associated with increases in angry responding. Finally, there was weak to negligible support for the notion that children are more likely to *model the same-sex parent*. Girls were more likely to model mother's than fathers' aggressive behaviors, but only one of eight analyses of this hypothesis were significant. Moreover, parent gender failed to moderate the link between interparental conflict and boys' aggressive behaviors in any of the analyses.

The notion that children are affected by marital conflict due to the presence of aggressive models has been long held (Emery, 1982) but has rarely been tested in relation to other theoretical accounts. Our findings suggest that processes other than modeling are important in understanding differences in children's reactions to parental conflict. The pattern of results corresponds well to the operation of distinct processes proposed in the emotional security hypothesis. For example, the finding that children are especially disturbed by child-related rather than adult-related themes (e.g., Block, Block, & Morrison, 1981; Grych, 1998; Grych & Fincham, 1993; Jouriles et al., 1991; Vaughn, Block, & Block, 1988) is not only consistent with earlier empirical results but is also explicitly hypothesized by the emotional security hypothesis (Davies & Cummings, 1994). Likewise, consistent with the emotional security hypothesis and one previous study (Laumakis et al., 1998), children reported feeling more distressed by threats to intactness than by general forms of verbal hostility.

Behavioral responses that are hypothesized to reflect modeling processes were also less likely to be endorsed by children than were emotional security processes reflecting efforts to regulate exposure to parental conflict. Thus, children more frequently reported avoiding or intervening in the conflict than imitating or experiencing dysregulation in response to parents' aggressive behaviors. Although the relatively high incidence of regulatory behaviors is consistent with previous studies (e.g., Cummings, Zahn-Waxler, & Radke-Yarrow, 1981; Davies & Cummings, 1998), earlier research commonly subsumed types of behavioral dysregulation within indices of regulation of conflict exposure. In disentangling reactions to exposure to parental conflict, this study is valuable in examining the relative prevalence of specific categories of behaviors.

An original contribution of this study emanates from tests of the different predictions about the relationship between changes in destructive conflict and changes in children's emotional responding. Whereas the emotional security hypothesis proposes that increases in the destructiveness of conflict processes are associated with corresponding increases in the child's fearful responding, social learning theory hypothesizes that exposure to more aggressive or destructive conflicts are associated with greater anger. Results of the analyses provided further support for the predictions of the emotional security hypothesis. Fearful, but not angry, responses increased as a function of exposure to more destructive, aggressive conflict between parents. Fear is among the most cogent indicators of insecurity. Thus, when interpreted in our theory, these findings suggest that exposure to more destructive forms of conflict increasingly undermines children's sense of security. Furthermore, these results more broadly illustrate the value of sharpening hypotheses and assessments to capture specific types of emotions rather than forms of undifferentiated, negative emotionality (Crockenberg & Langrock, 2001a, 2001b).

In one of the few specific tests of children's responding to mothers' versus fathers' conflict tactics, only weak support emerged for modeling hypotheses about child reactions being influenced by parental gender. The finding that girls were more likely to model mothers' than fathers' physical aggression toward an object must be weighed against the number of nonsignificant tests for girls and boys. Although the null findings are not inconsistent with the emotional security hypothesis or other theories like the cognitive-contextual framework, they do fail to support hypotheses offered by social learning theory and other conceptualizations, such as specific emotions theory (Crockenberg & Langrock, 2001a).

However, in this study, we selectively identified a subset of research questions that maximized differences between the two theories in generating hypotheses. Consideration of the more comprehensive set of predictions outlined by social learning theory will likely continue to illustrate its usefulness in understanding children's responses to conflict (Crockenberg & Forgays, 1996; Crockenberg & Langrock, 2001a). Furthermore, modeling theories, which distinguish between acquisition and performance stages of learning, argue that children may learn behaviors through witnessing adult aggression but may delay endorsing or performing the behaviors for a considerable time after exposure. Thus, our focus on children's immediate responses may underestimate the role of modeling in children's exposure to conflict.

The primary goal of this study was to examine how well a subset of predictions derived from the emotional security hypothesis fared relative to a subset of predictions derived from other theories of interparental conflict. The results provide promising support for the relative utility of the emotional security hypothesis in relation to another theory.

III. STUDY 2: RELATIONS BETWEEN INTERPARENTAL CONFLICT, CHILD EMOTIONAL SECURITY, AND ADJUSTMENT IN THE CONTEXT OF COGNITIVE APPRAISALS

The cognitive-contextual framework (Grych & Fincham, 1990) and the emotional security hypothesis (Davies & Cummings, 1994) present two explanations for why interparental conflict is thought to directly affect child psychological adjustment. The two theories provide remarkably similar predictions regarding the mechanisms that account for the association between histories of exposure to parental conflict and child maladjustment. Both theories predict that the child responds with progressively more negative affect and cognitions when repeatedly exposed to destructive marital conflict (e.g., Davies et al., 1999). Moreover, the common hypothesis is that this greater sensitization leads to increases in the child's risk for adjustment problems. Thus, there is some correspondence between the theories in their conceptualization of emotions and appraisals as mediators of interparental conflict. The goal of this study is to compare and contrast the specific types of response processes that are proposed to account for the relationship between interparental conflict and child adjustment in the emotional security hypothesis and cognitive-contextual framework.

Despite the similarities, important differences exist between the theories in their emphasis on central response processes in the child that mediate associations between parental conflict and child adjustment. The cognitive-contextual framework emphasizes the central role of the child's cognitive appraisals of the meaning of conflict in understanding why interparental conflict leads to increases in the child's vulnerability to adjustment problems. Self-blame and perceived threat are specifically hypothesized to be fundamental mechanisms that mediate interparental conflict. Not only have these specific types of appraisals been valuable in assessing the dynamics of interparental conflict from the child's perspective (e.g., Cummings, Davies, et al., 1994; Grych et al., 1992; Kerig, 1998b), but empirical evidence indicates that perceived threat and self-blame mediate relations between the child's perceptions of destructive conflict properties and child adjustment (Grych, Fincham, et al., 2000).

In contrast, the emotional security hypothesis emphasizes that children evaluate interparental conflict in relation to the implications it has for their emotional security. Emotions are assumed to play a primary role in the context of histories of experiences with interparental conflict, the child's broader patterns of reactivity to conflict, and subsequent child adjustment patterns. Difficulties in preserving emotional security are hypothesized to stem from repeated exposure to hostile, threatening conflict between parents, and these difficulties, in turn, increase a child's risk for adjustment problems. Emotional security, however, is a latent goal. Thus, difficulties in achieving the goal of security must be inferred from three interdependent response classes consisting of emotional reactivity, regulation of exposure to conflict (i.e., involvement, avoidance), and hostile internal representations of parental conflict. Like the cognitive contextual-framework, the limited research examining links between interparental conflict and child adjustment has provided support for the notion that the three response classes may account, in part, for associations between parental conflict and child adjustment (e.g., Davies & Cummings, 1998; Davies et al., 2002).

Although studies have offered initial support for the mediating role of the child's cognitive appraisals and emotional security processes proposed in each theory, methodological and conceptual characteristics of these studies have limited advances in theory testing. At a methodological level, the studies have relied on cross-sectional designs in testing the mediational role of cognitive appraisals and emotional security (e.g., Davies & Cummings, 1998; Grych, Fincham, et al., 2000). Demonstrating concurrent associations between the proposed mediator (i.e., cognitive appraisals, emotional insecurity) and the outcome (i.e., adjustment problems) in path or structural equation models (SEMs) cannot address the possibility that adjustment problems are actually affecting children's cognitive appraisals and emotional insecurity rather than vice versa. Experiencing internalizing and externalizing symptoms may prime the child to subsequent conflicts in a way that increases perceptions of threat, appraisals of self-blame, and a sense of insecurity. Moreover, *trait negative affectivity*, which is defined as the tendency to experience high levels of psychological distress irrespective of the presence of overt stress, may be a third variable that artificially inflates weak or negligible associations between conflict reactivity and child adjustment (Harold & Conger, 1997). Because individuals with high levels of trait negative affectivity experience more dissatisfaction and negative appraisals of themselves and others, Watson and Pennebaker (1989) have cogently argued that high levels of trait negative affectivity may influence reports of *trait level* variables like psychological adjustment and of more dynamic *state level* variables like child appraisals and reaction patterns to conflict.

At a conceptual level, hypotheses derived from the emotional security hypothesis and the cognitive-contextual framework have commonly been examined in isolation from each other (e.g., Davies & Cummings, 1998; Grych et al., 2000). Likewise, studies designed to simultaneously examine the validity of the emotional security hypothesis and the cognitive-contextual framework tend to examine hypotheses that are common to both theories (e.g., Davies et al., 1999). In calling attention to this issue in the literature, Fincham, Grych, and Osborne (1994) noted that studies have predominantly tested single conceptual models against the null hypothesis. Although they recommended that advances in this area will hinge on testing the relative empirical fit of theoretically guided models in relation to other plausible conceptual models (also see Cummings, Goeke-Morey, Dukewich, 2001), the literature to date has failed to heed this call.

Therefore, the purpose of the present report is to provide the first test of the relative roles of cognitive-contextual and emotional security processes as mediators in the link between interparental conflict and child adjustment. Guided by the predictions of these theories, SEMs were specified to test the mediating roles of perceived threat, self-blame, and emotional security in links between interparental conflict histories and child internalizing and externalizing symptoms. Valid and reliable child self-report measures of cognitive-contextual appraisals (Children's Perception of Interparental Conflict Scale, CPIC; Grych et al., 1992) and children's insecurity (Security in the Interparental Subsystem Scale, SIS; Davies et al., 2002) provide bases for developing psychometrically fair tests of the relative roles of the different response processes. Therefore, this study utilized these measures in testing perceived threat, self-blame, and emotional insecurity as mediators of parental conflict. Furthermore, to reduce the plausibility of methodological explanations for the findings (e.g., cause-effect relations running from adjustment problems to child emotional or cognitive responses, with trait negative affectivity as a third variable), a two-wave, prospective design was utilized with measurement occasions spaced two years apart. Measures of interparental conflict at Time 1 and the three mediators at Time 2 were specified as predictors of adjustment problems at Time 2 after controlling for Time 1 adjustment problems.

Although formulating definitive hypotheses would be premature in the context of limited research, the theory guiding this study provided a basis for offering some tentative predictions. Figure 2 summarizes the tentative predictions of primary interest in testing the theories. First, child emotional insecurity in the interparental relationship, as reflected in emotional reactivity, regulation of exposure to parental conflict, and negative

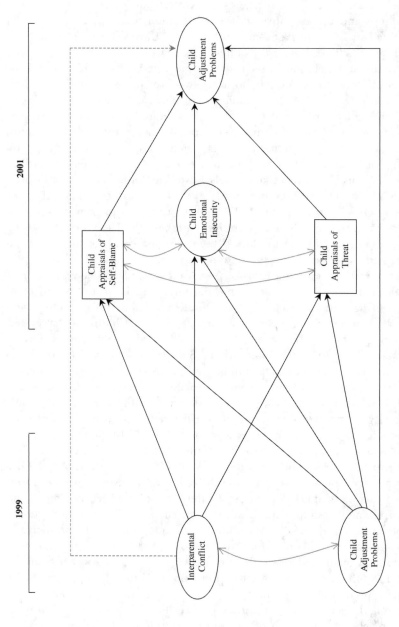

FIGURE 2.—A conceptual model of emotional security and cognitive-contextual appraisals as intervening mechanisms in the link between interparental conflict and child psychological functioning.

internal representations is hypothesized to mediate the association between interparental conflict histories and adjustment problems. Thus, interparental conflict is hypothesized to be associated with greater insecurity in the context of interparental conflict, which, in turn, is assumed to be related to child adjustment problems, particularly in the form of internalizing symptoms. If these pathways are robust, as the emotional security hypothesis suggests, emotional security will also continue to account for associations between parental conflict and child adjustment even after taking into account the mediational role of perceived threat and self-blame. Second, given the significance of the cognitive-contextual framework as a heuristic for research, we also hypothesize that perceived threat and self-blame mediate or account, in part, for associations between interparental conflict and child adjustment even after taking into account the mediating role of emotional insecurity. Thus, interparental conflict is proposed to be related to perceived threat and self-blame, which, in turn, is expected to be linked with greater adjustment problems. Third, despite some important distinctions made in the specific response processes that are hypothesized to serve as mediators, the central response processes of children in the two theories share a considerable degree of conceptual overlap. Therefore, it is hypothesized that perceived threat, self-blame, and emotional insecurity are related rather than independent. Finally, both models are midlevel theories that are not designed to explain all of the risk posed by interparental conflict. Thus, in light of the significance of other processes as mediators (see Margolin et al., 2001), the dotted lines denote that interparental conflict may continue to be associated with child adjustment problems even after delineating the mediating effects of the cognitive and emotional mechanisms.

METHOD

Participants

The data for these analyses were taken from the same longitudinal study of Welsh families used in Study 1. Given the primary focus on interparental conflict, children were included in this study if (a) the child lived with at least one biological parent and another male or female guardian and (b) both the parents and children completed all the measures of interparental discord, appraisals of threat and self-blame, emotional security, and child adjustment. These criteria yielded a sample of 285 children and parents (139 boys and 146 girls). Although this sample of families overlapped considerably with the sample used in Study 1, the two samples were not identical for two primary reasons. First, due to delays in funding, only 218 of 285 children who completed questionnaires for the longitudinal study participated in the analogue procedures of Study 1. Thus, some children who did not participate in the analogue study were included in this study because they completed the relevant survey measures. Second, approximately 71% of parents of participating children completed and returned their questionnaires during the first year of assessment. Consequently, some children who participated in Study 1 (which only required child participants) were excluded from the present study because complete data were not available for parent and child reports of family measures. Third, due to the attrition rate of 28% from the first (1999) to second (2001) measurement occasion, additional families who participated in the analogue study did not meet the criteria for participating in the current study.

Despite these differences, demographic statistics suggest that the sample is representative of British families living in the U.K. region of England and Wales with regard to family constitution, ethnic representation, economic diversity, and parent education (Social Trends, 2002). Moreover, three sets of statistical analyses supported the notion that the samples of children were not statistically distinguishable from each other for any of the variables of primary interest in this study: (a) child participants whose parents completed the survey batteries did not significantly differ from child participants whose parents did not complete the surveys, (b) children who participated in the analogue procedures did not differ from children who did not participate in the analogue procedures, and (c) families who attrited did not differ from families who participated in both measurement occasions.

The vast majority of the children in the current sample lived with both biological parents (89.5%); the remaining children lived with their biological mother and stepfather (9.1%) or biological father and stepmother (1.4%). Thirty-seven percent of mothers and 32.6% of fathers had completed secondary or high-school education only, 32.9% of mothers and 30.3% of fathers had completed technical or vocational level training, and 30.2% of mothers and 37.1% of fathers had completed university education. The ethnicity of the vast majority of children was White–European (99%), followed by small proportions of other ethnic groups (0.5% Indian, Sri-Lankan, and 0.5% other, including East African, Jamaican). Children, who were recruited from nine schools, ranged in age from 11 to 13 years, with a mean age of 11.67 years in the first year of the study.

Procedure

After receiving permission from area schools to conduct the study, parents were informed about the study by written summaries sent through the mail and presentations at parent-teacher meetings. Children whose parents completed the consent forms completed their questionnaires during the course of the school day. Teachers also completed questionnaires assessing child psychological functioning. Parents who indicated an interest in participating in the study were sent questionnaire packets to complete and return in postage-free envelopes. No payment was made to families, but parents were informed that a summary booklet outlining key research findings would be distributed to all families upon completion of the study.

Measures

Interparental conflict. Mothers and fathers completed two measures of interparental functioning designed to assess general interparental distress and overt discord. The Short Marital Adjustment Test, which assesses overall interparental adjustment and consensus, has excellent reliability and discriminant validity (SMAT; Locke & Wallace, 1959; also see Fincham, Beach, Harold & Osborne, 1997). Parent responses were coded so that higher scores reflected greater interparental distress. Internal consistency estimates for the current sample were $\alpha = .87$ for husbands and $\alpha = .82$ for wives. Mother and father responses were summed together to form a single composite of interparental distress ($\alpha = .80$).

Overt interparental discord was assessed using a scale specifically developed for this study. The measure consists of 10 items reflecting interparental management of conflict (e.g., "Our arguments end up with one or both of us feeling hurt or angry" and "Our arguments end with an exchange of insults"). Response alternatives range from 1 = *almost never* to 5 = *almost always*. Alpha coefficients for the scale items were .87 and .88 for fathers and mothers, respectively. Mother and father responses were summed to form a single measure of interparental conflict ($\alpha = .91$).

Child appraisals of self-blame and threat. Child appraisals of threat and self-blame were measured by the Perceived Threat and Self-Blame subscales of the CPIC (Grych et al., 1992). Eleven items comprise the Threat scale and include items indexing the child's worries about the implications of conflict (e.g., "When my parents argue I worry what will happen to me") and confidence in the ability to cope with conflicts (e.g., "When my parents argue I can do something to make myself feel better"). Due to concerns raised during the process of obtaining ethical approval for the study, one item, "When my parents argue I'm afraid one of them will get hurt," was omitted from the scale. Nine items comprise the Self-Blame scale and include items such as "It is usually my fault when my parents argue" and "My parents blame me when they have arguments." Evidence for the reliability and different forms of validity (e.g., discriminant, convergent) are well-established (Grych et al., 1992; Grych, Fincham, et al., 2000; Grych, Jouriles, Swank, McDonald, & Norwood, 2000). Three items ("When my parents argue I worry that they might split up," "When my parents argue I am afraid that something bad will happen," and "I get scared when my parents argue") evidenced considerable overlap with items indexing child insecurity. Given that these items primarily tap child emotional responses rather than cognitive responses, the items were dropped from the CPIC to preserve the focus on emotions and fear in the measures of emotional security. Both measures evidenced good internal consistency ($\alpha = .72$ and $.84$ for Perceived Threat and Self-Blame, respectively). Moreover, when the three items were retained as part of the Perceived Threat scale and dropped from the emotional security measures, results of the primary analyses (i.e., SEMs) were highly similar.

Child emotional security in the context of interparental conflict. The three component processes of child emotional security in the context of interparental conflict were measured by child reports on the SIS (Davies et al., 2002). First, emotional reactivity was assessed by the Emotional Reactivity subscale. The 12 items on the subscale are designed to assess multiple, prolonged, and dysregulated expressions of fear and distress (e.g., "When my parents argue I feel scared," "When my parents argue, it ruins my whole day"). Second, regulation of exposure to conflict was assessed by summing 12 items from the Avoidance and Involvement subscales of the SIS. The Involvement subscale assesses the child's emotional and behavioral involvement in conflicts (e.g., "When my parents have an argument, I try to solve the problem for them"), whereas the Avoidance subscale measures the child's efforts to escape from or avoid interparental conflict or its adverse aftermath (e.g., "When my parents have an argument, I keep really still almost as if I was frozen"). Third, items from Destructive Family Representations, Conflict Spillover Representations, and Constructive Representations (reverse scored) subscales of the SIS were summed together to form a measure of internal representations of interparental relations. Alpha coefficients for the composites of emotional reactivity, regulation of conflict exposure, and internal representations were .87, .77, and .87, respectively.

Child psychological adjustment. Measures of internalizing symptoms and externalizing problems were obtained to assess child psychological maladjustment. Because children tend to be the most accurate reporters of their internalizing symptoms (Achenbach, 1991), children reported on their internalizing symptoms by completing the Children's Depression Inventory (CDI; Kovacs, 1981) and the Depression-Anxiety and Withdrawn subscales from the Youth Self-Report (YSR) form of the Child Behavior Checklist (CBCL; Achenbach, 1991). One item tapping suicidal thoughts was omitted from the CDI. Support for the reliability and validity of both the CDI (Harold et al., 1997; Kovacs, 1981) and the CBCL (Achenbach, 1991; Davies et al., 2002) is well documented. Sample items from the CBCL include "I cry a lot," "I feel lonely," and "I am too fearful or anxious," whereas the CDI contains items such as "I feel alone all the time," "I am sad all the time," and "All bad things are my fault." Items from these measures are scored on scales that range from 0 to 2. Each measure of internalizing provided acceptable estimates of internal reliability at both time points in this sample: α = .86 and .88 for the CDI; α = .81 and .89 for the CBCL Depression-Anxiety subscale; α = .51 and .69 for the CBCL Withdrawn subscale.

Child externalizing symptoms were assessed by teacher and child reports of externalizing behaviors using the child reports on the externalizing scale of the YSR form of the CBCL (Achenbach, 1991) and the Buss and Durkee (1957) trait measure of antisocial behavior. Teachers also completed the externalizing scale from the Teacher Report Form (TRF) of the CBCL (Achenbach, 1991). Different teachers completed questionnaires for children at each time point across the study period (r = .48, $p < .01$). Items from the YSR and TRF externalizing scales assess behaviors such as "Argues a lot," "Has a hot temper or throws temper tantrums," and "Threatens to hurt others." The Buss and Durkee measure contains questions such has, "When I get angry I say nasty things" and "When people shout at me, I shout back." Good reliability estimates were demonstrated for this sample for each of these measures of children's externalizing behavior at both time points (teacher report of aggression, α = .94 and .95; child report of aggression, α = .84 and .86; antisocial behavior, α = .83 and .83).

RESULTS

Preliminary Analyses

Table 2 contains the means, standard deviations, and intercorrelations for all variables used as indicators of constructs in testing the theoretical model. In support of the measurement model, moderate to strong associations were found among the proposed indicators of marital conflict (r (285) = .58), appraisals of self-blame and threat (r (285) = .44), emotional security (mean r (285) = .54), internalizing symptoms (mean r (285) = .45 and .63 at Times 1 and 2, respectively), and externalizing symptoms, (r (285) = .42 and .39 at Times 1 and 2, respectively).

Table 3 provides the correlations among the latent constructs used in the primary analyses. Consistent with some previous studies using parent reports of interparental conflict (Harold & Conger, 1997; Harold et al.,

TABLE 2

INTERCORRELATIONS AMONG INDICATORS OF PARENTAL DISCORD, CHILD REACTIVITY TO CONFLICT, AND CHILD PSYCHOLOGICAL SYMPTOMS

Variables	1	2	3	4	5	6	7	8	9	10	11	12	13	14	15	16	17	18	M	SD
Time 1 (1999) Parental discord																				
1. Interparental distress (P)	—																		61.54	33.74
2. Interparental discord (P)	.58	—																	37.76	12.09
Time 1 (1999) Child psychological symptoms																				
3. Withdrawal (C)	.02	.04	—																2.81	1.88
4. Anxiety-depression (C)	.05	.05	.52	—															6.08	4.08
5. Depression (C)	.08	.06	.35	.48	—														8.84	6.85
6. Aggression (C)	.08	.06	.24	.38	.40	—													8.85	5.58
7. Antisocial behavior (C)	.10	.09	.09	.10	.25	.60	—												23.29	7.34
8. Aggression (T)	.03	.00	.04	.01	.10	.35	.31	—											2.68	5.65
Time 2 (2001) Child reactivity to conflict																				
9. Self-blame (C)	.09	.11	.00	.03	.25	.18	.10	.15	—										12.30	3.79
10. Perceived threat (C)	.11	.14	.11	.29	.28	.15	.07	.04	.44	—									13.14	3.28
11. Emotional reactivity (C)	.08	.14	.14	.30	.29	.22	.13	.07	.39	.61	—								21.13	6.80
12. Regulation of conflict (C)	.03	.06	.13	.23	.12	.05	.05	.02	.16	.40	.59	—							26.65	6.04
13. Internal representations (C)	.14	.23	.00	.18	.29	.14	.10	.14	.47	.58	.68	.36	—						19.78	6.61
Time 2 (2001) Child psychological symptoms																				
14. Withdrawal (C)	.06	.07	.42	.31	.26	.10	.06	.07	.09	.21	.33	.23	.15	—					2.94	2.34
15. Anxiety-depression (C)	.01	.05	.28	.51	.36	.16	.03	.12	.20	.39	.52	.36	.36	.67	—				5.93	5.22
16. Depression (C)	.06	.12	.22	.36	.55	.27	.13	.04	.40	.39	.50	.22	.46	.53	.69	—			9.90	7.59
17. Aggression (C)	.11	.11	.15	.23	.38	.52	.41	.21	.34	.24	.35	.16	.32	.32	.43	.49	—		9.40	5.95
18. Antisocial behavior (C)	.14	.10	.05	.03	.17	.35	.52	.22	.29	.11	.23	.07	.24	.09	.03	.24	.63	—	23.77	7.02
19. Aggression (T)	.06	.06	.03	.01	.17	.32	.25	.48	.33	.09	.06	.04	.20	.04	.03	.14	.28	.26	2.94	5.83

Note.—P = parent-report measure; T = teacher-report measure; C = child-report measure.
$r \geq .12$, $p < .05$; $r \geq .15$, $p < .01$.

TABLE 3

INTERCORRELATIONS AMONG THE LATENT CONSTRUCTS USED
IN THE STRUCTURAL EQUATION MODELS

Variables	1	2	3	4	5	6	7
1. Interparental conflict	—						
2. Internalizing symptoms (Time 1)	.09	—					
3. Externalizing symptoms (Time 1)	.10	.49*	—				
4. Self-blame appraisals	.13$^+$	.10	.19*	—			
5. Perceived threat	.16*	.34*	.15*	.44*	—		
6. Emotional insecurity	.19*	.38*	.23*	.45*	.68*	—	
7. Internalizing symptoms (Time 2)	.08	.65*	.21*	.26*	.42*	.61*	—
8. Externalizing symptoms (Time 2)	.15*	.34*	.61*	.37*	.25*	.40*	.50*

Note.—$^+p < .10$; *$p < .05$.

1997), interparental conflict failed to predict child adjustment problems at either time point. Thus, because demonstrating mediation requires demonstrating that the predictor and outcome be significantly associated, these findings indicate that emotional security and cognitive-contextual variables cannot serve as mediators. However, these variables may still act as processes that link interparental conflict and child maladjustment. To test whether interparental conflict is indirectly associated with child maladjustment through its association with child responses to conflict, it is first necessary to demonstrate significant associations between (a) interparental conflict and child responses to conflict, and (b) child responses to conflict and their psychological symptoms. Supporting these criteria, interparental conflict was associated with self-blame, perceived threat, and emotional insecurity. Each of these three processes, in turn, was related to child internalizing and externalizing symptoms (see Table 3).

Structural Equation Analysis of the Overall Model

Structural equation modeling using maximum likelihood estimation was employed to test the proposed theoretical model (LISREL 8.50; Joreskog & Sorbom, 1996). The model outlined in Figure 1 was first specified separately for boys and girls. Subgroup comparisons revealed no significant gender differences in the models predicting internalizing or externalizing symptoms. Therefore, for the sake of maximizing power, parsimony, and generalizability, boys and girls were combined in the primary analyses.

Figures 3 and 4 contain the results for the test of the overall model predicting child internalizing and externalizing symptoms, respectively. The chi-squares for the models and goodness-of-fit indices suggest that these

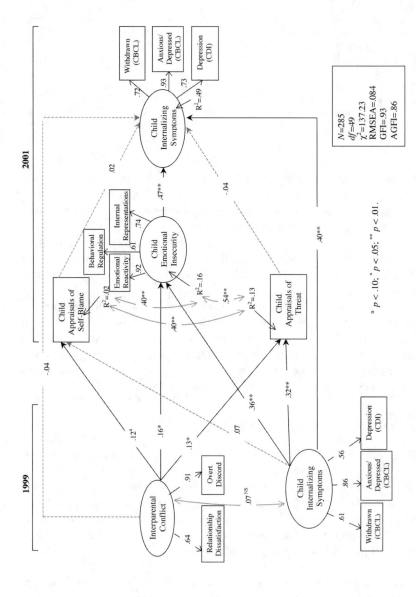

FIGURE 3.—A structural equation model testing the role of child emotional security and cognitive-contextual appraisals in accounting for links between interparental conflict and child internalizing symptoms.

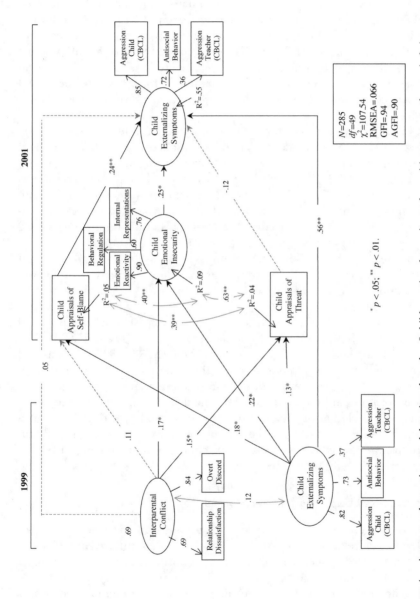

FIGURE 4.—A structural equation model testing the role of child emotional security and cognitive-contextual appraisals in accounting for links between interparental conflict and child externalizing problems.

models provide a good fit to the data (internalizing: $\chi^2_{49} = 137.23$, GFI = .93, AGFI = .86, RMSEA = .084; externalizing: $\chi^2_{49} = 109.19$, GFI = .94, AGFI = .90, RMSEA = .066). In support of the measurement portion of the model, indicator loadings for each of the latent constructs included in the model (excluding externalizing symptoms) were statistically significant and relatively strong in magnitude (loadings ranged from .60 to .93). The indicator loadings for teacher reports of child externalizing symptoms were statistically significant but lower than the general range of loadings across the model ($\lambda = .37$ and .36). However, teacher reports of child behavioral problems were retained to remedy the potential for analyses to be biased by reliance on child reports of all endogenous measures included in the model.

In examining the structural part of the model, interparental conflict was significantly associated with child appraisals of threat and emotional security in models of internalizing and externalizing symptoms even after controlling for the effects of Time 1 symptoms on children's responses (β ranged from .13 to .17, $p < .05$). Child emotional security and cognitive appraisals, in turn, were associated with internalizing and externalizing symptoms. Emotional security was associated with both internalizing ($\beta = .47$, $p < .01$) and externalizing ($\beta = .25$, $p < .05$) symptoms. Although self-blame was linked with externalizing symptoms ($\beta = .24$, $p < .05$), it failed to predict internalizing symptoms. Moreover, perceived threat was not significantly associated with either form of child psychological symptomatology.

Overall, these findings indicate that interparental conflict was linked with the child's subsequent psychological symptoms through its association with the child's emotional insecurity even when initial symptoms and cognitive appraisals were considered in the same model. By contrast, cognitive appraisals were not found to be robust intervening processes in the models of interparental conflict when initial symptoms and emotional security were included in the analyses. However, moderate to strong correlations between emotional insecurity and cognitive appraisals suggest that cognitive appraisals are associated with child symptoms through their association with emotional insecurity.

Comparisons of Competing Theoretical Models

To further test the validity of our proposed theoretical model, we examined its relative empirical fit in relation to alternative, nested models (Bollen, 1989). Because the chi-square statistic is an index of the magnitude of the difference between the theoretical model specified in the SEM and the actual data, it is possible to examine whether adding specific paths in the model results in significant improvements in the fit of the theoretical model (i.e., significant reductions in the chi-square statistic). Figure 5 depicts the specific paths estimated in each of the models and Table 4 presents the results of comparisons of the relative fit of these different models.

Paths labeled "1" in Figure 5 denote the paths that were estimated in Model 1 (i.e., the baseline model). Accordingly, the following paths were estimated in Model 1: (a) interparental conflict and child symptoms at Times 1 and 2; (b) Time 1 symptoms and child appraisals of threat, self-blame, and emotional insecurity; and (c) Time 1 and Time 2 symptoms. The association between child appraisals of self-blame and threat was also specified in the model. Paths that were not estimated included associations between interparental conflict and the three child response variables, the child response variables and Time 2 symptoms, and emotional security and the two types of appraisals. Thus, this analysis examines the overall fit of a model where the indirect paths between interparental conflict, child conflict reactivity, and child symptoms are not specified.

To examine the fit of the cognitive-contextual framework, Model 2a not only estimates all the paths in Model 1 (the paths labeled "1" in Figure 1), but also specifies additional paths between (a) interparental conflict and child appraisals of self-blame and threat, and (b) child appraisals of threat and self-blame and Time 2 child symptoms (the paths labeled "2a" in Figure 1). Notably, without considering emotional security in the model, significant associations are found between (a) self-blame and child internalizing ($\beta = .12$, $p < .05$) and externalizing ($\beta = .29$, $p < .01$) symptoms and (b) perceived threat and child internalizing symptoms ($\beta = .21$, $p < .05$). In evaluating the overall fit of the model of internalizing symptoms, there was no significant reduction in the chi-square index when the cognitive-contextual paths are added to the baseline model of internalizing symptoms ($\Delta\chi^2 = 5.67$, $\Delta df = 4$). These findings suggest that incorporating child appraisals of threat and self-blame as intervening processes between interparental conflict and child internalizing symptoms does not improve the fit between the theoretical model and the data beyond the paths specified in the baseline model (Model 1). In contrast, a different pattern of results was found for the model of externalizing symptoms. Moving from the baseline model to the cognitive-contextual model resulted in a significant reduction in the chi-square statistics ($\Delta\chi^2 = 30.09$, $\Delta df = 4$). These findings suggest that incorporating paths hypothesized in the cognitive-contextual framework does add significant explanatory power to models of interparental conflict and child externalizing symptoms when measured two years later.

To examine the relative fit of the emotional security model in relation to the baseline model, Model 2b not only estimated paths in Model 1 (i.e., Paths 1 in Figure 5), but also added the following paths: (a) interparental

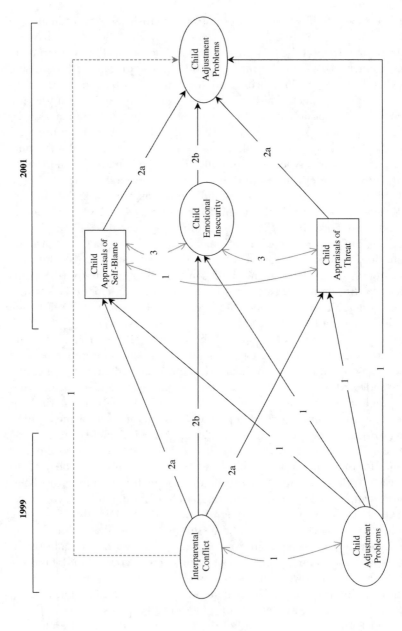

FIGURE 5. —A conceptual illustration of the alternative analytic models specified for testing associations between interparental conflict, child appraisals and emotional security, and psychological symptoms.

TABLE 4

Comparison of the Relative Empirical Fit of Theoretical Models
Involving Appraisals and Emotional Security

Estimated Model	Internalizing Symptoms				Externalizing Symptoms			
	χ^2	df	$\Delta\chi^2$	Δdf	χ^2	df	$\Delta\chi^2$	Δdf
Model 1: Baseline	271.81	57	—	—	285.47	57	—	—
Model 2a: Cognitive-contextual	266.14	53	5.67^{ns}	4	255.38	53	30.09*	4
Model 2b: Emotional security	261.14	55	10.67*	2	271.07	55	14.40*	2
Model 3: Integrated	137.23	49	128.91* (2a)	4	107.54	49	147.84* (2a)	4
			123.91* (2b)	6			163.53* (2b)	6

Note—*$\Delta\chi^2/\Delta df = p < .05$.

conflict and children's emotional insecurity, and (b) children's emotional insecurity and psychological symptoms (i.e., Paths 2b in Figure 5). Significant associations were found between interparental conflict and emotional insecurity (β = .12, p < .05) and emotional insecurity and each form of maladjustment (internalizing, β = .42, p < .01; externalizing, β = .23, p < .05). In contrast to the cognitive-contextual framework, the addition of these emotional security paths resulted in significant reductions in the chi-square statistic for models of internalizing ($\Delta\chi^2$ = 10.67, Δdf = 2, p < .05) and externalizing ($\Delta\chi^2$ = 14.40, Δdf = 2, p < .05) symptoms. Thus, including indirect pathways between interparental conflict, emotional insecurity, and each form of maladjustment significantly improved the explanatory power of the model relative to the baseline model.

Model 3 was designed to test a model that integrates paths proposed in both the emotional security hypothesis and cognitive-contextual framework in a single model. In addition to estimating paths contained in Model 1 (i.e., Paths 1 in Figure 5), it also specifies paths contained in Models 2a and 2b (Paths 2a and 2b in Figure 5) and associations between child appraisals of threat and self-blame and their emotional security (all Paths 3 in Figure 5). Model 3 provided a significantly better representation of the data than did Model 2a ($\Delta\chi^2$ = 128.91, Δdf = 4, p < .05 for internalizing symptoms; $\Delta\chi^2$ = 147.84, Δdf = 4, p < .05, for externalizing symptoms) or Model 2b ($\Delta\chi^2$ = 123.91, Δdf = 6, p < .05 for internalizing symptoms; $\Delta\chi^2$ = 163.53, Δdf = 6, p < .05, for externalizing symptoms). Thus, the results indicate that the model that integrates the key propositions of the emotional security hypothesis and the cognitive-contextual framework provides a more complete account of the mechanisms explaining associations between interparental conflict and child adjustment than either theory considered singly.

DISCUSSION

Both the emotional security hypothesis and the cognitive-contextual framework provide accounts of child processes that intervene between interparental conflict and child maladjustment (Davies & Cummings, 1994; Grych & Fincham, 1990). In an attempt to integrate the emotional security hypothesis and the cognitive-contextual framework, this chapter examined the relative roles of child emotional security and cognitive appraisals of threat and self-blame in accounting for links between interparental conflict and long-term child maladjustment. In support of the emotional security hypothesis, the results indicated that child emotional security in the context of interparental conflict is a key intervening process that links interparental discord with subsequent child internalizing and externalizing symptoms even when cognitive-contextual mechanisms are considered in the same analytic models. In particular, parental discord was associated with child insecurity two years later. Emotional insecurity, in turn, was associated with concurrent internalizing and externalizing symptoms even after controlling for internalizing and externalizing symptoms two years earlier.

Consistent with previous research (e.g., Grych, Fincham, Jouriles, et al., 2000), appraisals of perceived threat and self-blame discussed within the cognitive-contextual framework were identified as important intervening processes that link interparental conflict and child maladjustment in analyses when emotional security is not included in the model. Interparental conflict was specifically associated with child internalizing symptoms through its link with perceived threat and self-blame. Likewise, interparental conflict was related to externalizing symptoms through its association with child appraisals of self-blame. However, these indirect pathways between interparental conflict, appraisals, and child maladjustment were no longer significant when emotional security was included in the analyses. More specifically, the two types of appraisals were generally unrelated to child adjustment problems when the significant associations between emotional security and child maladjustment were estimated. In addition to lending further support to the assumption that emotional security is a robust process that links interparental conflict with child maladjustment, the findings suggest (albeit speculatively) that emotional security may account for part of the pathways between interparental conflict, appraisals, and adjustment in the cognitive-contextual framework.

However, for several reasons, our findings should not be interpreted as failing to support the cognitive-contextual framework. First, many of the hypotheses and theoretical constructs in the emotional security hypothesis and cognitive-contextual framework are very similar. For example, associations between emotional security and child appraisals (especially perceived threat) in this study were moderate in magnitude, thereby suggesting considerable conceptual overlap. Likewise, when analyzed in isolation from each other, emotional security and the two types of cognitive appraisals appeared to play similar roles in models of interparental conflict and child maladjustment. By virtue of the appreciable overlap between these theories, marshaling support for one theory does provide some support for the other theory.

Second, attesting to the value of integrating the theories, including both emotional security and cognitive appraisals as intervening variables in the models of interparental conflict and child psychological symptoms provided a significantly better representation of the data than considering either set of processes (i.e., emotional security or appraisals) alone. An important message of these results is that processes described by both theories appear to play a unique and mutually informative role in understanding associations between interparental conflict and specific forms of child maladjustment. Although caution must be exercised in drawing conclusions about directionality among variables, the findings of the integrative model are also consistent with the idea that child appraisals of threat and self-blame play an important role in the development of child maladjustment by undermining child feelings of security.

Third, conceptual overlap between the response processes outlined in the two theories merits consideration. The child's subjective evaluations of threat as articulated in the cognitive-contextual framework are consistent with processes of emotional insecurity in the emotional security hypothesis (Davies & Cummings, 1994). In particular, the emotional security hypothesis postulates that interparental conflict increases child vulnerability to adjustment problems by posing a threat to the well-being of the child and his or her family. In capturing child worries about their well-being in contexts of parental conflict, perceptions of threat in the cognitive-contextual framework constitute a specific goal that is pertinent to the broader, overarching goal of preserving emotional security in the emotional security hypothesis. Perceptions of threat are evaluated as one component in a larger goal system of preserving emotional security. Subsuming more specific threats within a broader, more holistic construct of emotional security is likely to increase its explanatory power in models of interparental conflict and child maladjustment.

The trade-off in conceptualizing emotional security as an aggregate of conceptually overlapping subgoals is a reduction in precision, especially in disentangling the specific relationships among parental conflict, specific response processes and goals, and child maladjustment. Thus, as Crockenberg and Langrock (2001a, 2001b) have cogently argued, an important complementary direction for research is to examine relations between interparental conflict, child functioning, and *specific* goals that are both within (e.g., worries about family dissolution, fears about being drawn into the conflict) and outside (e.g., being able to engage in activities, having a say in family decision-making processes) the conceptual boundaries of emotional security. Therefore, if perceived threat is conceptualized as reflecting difficulties with a *specific* goal of feeling protected in the family, the specific focus on perceived threat in the cognitive contextual framework can be considered an important step toward increasing the specificity in analyses of various, specific goals.

Fourth, the considerable explanatory power of emotional security in the models of interparental conflict may be an artifact of differences in the psychometric properties of measures of emotional security (SIS) and cognitive appraisals (CPIC). Although the validity and reliability of the Security in the Interparental Subsystem (Davies et al., 2002) and Children's Perceptions of Interparental Conflict (Grych et al., 1992) scales are well-established, it is possible that the SIS provides a more valid, comprehensive assessment than the CPIC of the primary constructs in the respective theories. In support of this interpretation, the cognitive-contextual framework also proposes that emotions, coping strategies, and other types of appraisals play an important role in understanding child responses to interparental conflict. However, assessments of these variables and their hypothesized roles (e.g., mediators, moderators, unique predictors) in associations between interparental and child functioning have yet to be developed (Holmbeck, 1997).

Some differences also emerged between the current findings and previous research on the emotional security hypothesis. A key assumption of the emotional security hypothesis is that interparental conflict directly affects child psychological maladjustment by undermining the child's emotional security. Marshaling support for this mediational pathway first requires establishing a link between interparental conflict and child maladjustment. However, interparental conflict was positively but not significantly associated with concurrent or prospective measures of child maladjustment. Differences between these findings and earlier empirical demonstrations of significant associations between interparental and child functioning may be attributable to the nonclinical nature of the sample or the reliance on a limited measurement battery for assessing interparental conflict (e.g., interparental dissatisfaction, new measure of interparental conflict). Although the findings did not lend support to the assumption that emotional security mediates the relationship between interparental conflict and child internalizing and externalizing symptoms, they did partly support the emotional security hypothesis in documenting that emotional security is an important intervening process that indirectly links interparental conflict and child maladjustment. That is, interparental conflict is linked with child adjustment problems indirectly through its association with child appraisals of self-blame, threat, and emotional insecurity. Although these findings did not replicate earlier empirical support for the mediational role of emotional security (e.g., Davies & Cummings, 1998), they are consistent with other empirical documentation of indirect pathways between interparental conflict and child maladjustment that utilize parent reports of conflict (e.g., Harold & Conger, 1997; Harold et al., 1997). More research is needed to enable a clear determination of whether pathways among parental conflict, child cognitive appraisals, emotional security, and different forms of psychological maladjustment are best characterized as mediating or indirect chains.

In summary, the results of this study suggest that emotional security plays an integral role in understanding pathways among parental conflict and child maladjustment. When interpreted in the context of our theoretical model in Chapter I (see Figure 1), the results provide support for the notion that witnessing destructive conflict between parents sensitizes child concerns about preserving security during bouts of conflict two years later. Significant associations between emotional security and maladjustment were also demonstrated even after controlling for child social-cognitive factors (i.e., appraisals of self-blame and threat) and initial levels of child maladjustment two years earlier.

IV. STUDY 3: PARENTAL CONFLICT AND CHILD SECURITY IN THE FAMILY SYSTEM

Although the findings from Studies 1 and 2 lend support to the significance of emotional security in relation to other theories of children's response processes, they do not address the role of other family processes in associations between interparental and child functioning. Guided by our conceptualization in Chapter I, this study specifically examines whether destructive interparental conflict and poor parenting practices are jointly associated with the child's difficulties in preserving emotional security in the context of interparental conflict and attachment insecurity in parent-child relationships. Figure 6 is presented to illustrate the possible pathways among the family factors (i.e., parental conflict, poor parenting), proposed mediators (i.e., emotional security, attachment security), and adjustment variables.

A primary assumption of the emotional security hypothesis is that child emotional insecurity in the context of interparental conflict is relatively distinct from child-parent attachment security in its substance, family correlates, and implications for child adjustment. In building on this assumption, child emotional security in the face of parental conflict is expected to mediate links between interparental conflict and psychological maladjustment even after taking into account the mediating role of parenting difficulties and child-parent attachment security (see Paths 1 and 6 in Figure 6).

Indirect effects models, which propose that parenting and parent-child relationship characteristics may account for associations between interparental conflict and child functioning, are especially relevant to providing a comprehensive analysis of the role of emotional security in the context of other family processes. Strong versions of indirect effects models pose a particular challenge to *direct effects* pathways in the emotional security hypothesis by proposing that parenting difficulties fully explain the link between interparental conflict and child adjustment (e.g., Erel et al., 1998; Fauber & Long, 1991). That is, this model directly questions the validity of the direct effects notion that interparental conflict is directly associated with children's coping and functioning. According to this model,

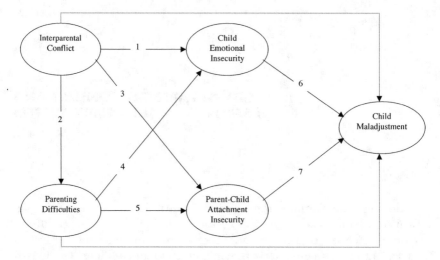

FIGURE 6.—A conceptual model of the joint interplay between interparental conflict and parenting difficulties in predicting child security in family relationships and psychological adjustment.

any mediational paths among interparental conflict, child emotional insecurity, and child maladjustment are fully explained or mediated by parenting processes. Thus, tests of the validity of the emotional security hypothesis must ultimately examine the plausibility of this competing hypothesis.

Weak versions of indirect effects models suggest that parenting and parent-child relationship processes only partly explain the link between interparental conflict and child maladjustment. Consistent with this model, a central assumption of the indirect effects pathway of the emotional security hypothesis is that the parent-child relationship accounts for part of the association between interparental conflict and child adjustment (Davies & Cummings, 1994). Although ample evidence suggests that parenting is a mediator of interparental conflict, the novel question raised in this family-wide model is whether this indirect effect remains robust when child emotional security in the family (i.e., interparental conflict, child-parent attachment security) is also considered. Attachment theory, for example, posits that parenting difficulties, especially in the form of emotional unavailability, increase the child's risk for developing adjustment problems by undermining the security of the child-parent attachment relationship (Belsky & Cassidy, 1994; Colin, 1996). In extending this assumption, the emotional security hypothesis further proposes that parenting difficulties accompanying interparental conflict are related to child adjustment problems through their association with child-parent attachment insecurity (see Paths 2, 5, and 7 in Figure 6). In support of part of this pathway, recent studies have demonstrated that dimensions of poor parenting partly mediate or account for the link between marital conflict and child-parent attachment security (e.g., Frosch et al., 2000; Owen & Cox, 1997). However, it is still not known whether child-parent attachment security, in turn, accounts for associations between poor parenting and child maladjustment in the context of interparental relationship processes.

Simultaneously examining child security in the context of interparental conflict and the parent-child attachment relationship also raises important questions about the relative magnitude of associations in pathways between forms of family difficulties, emotional security in different family relationships, and forms of child maladjustment. One important question relates to whether child emotional security across different relationships (i.e., interparental, parent-child attachment) is explained by experiential histories within that particular relationship or experiential histories across multiple family relationships. Thus, as an exploratory aim, we examine the specificity and generality of paths between interparental and parenting difficulties and child emotional security in the contexts of interparental conflicts and child-parent attachment relationships (Paths 1, 3, 4, and 5 in Figure 6). One hypothesis, which we label the *predictor specificity hypothesis*, proposes that child insecurity in a specific family relationship may develop in large part from the child's experiences within the specific relationship. It is possible that interparental conflict histories uniquely predict child emotional security in the context of interparental conflict, whereas poor parenting practices may specifically undermine child attachment security in the parent-child relationship (Cummings & Davies, 1996; Davies & Cummings, 1994). Alternatively, other work suggests that experiences within specific family relationships may predict security across multiple family relationships. For example, findings by Owen and Cox (1997) support the hypothesis that witnessing parents' frightening and frightened behavior during bouts of destructive parental conflict may directly compromise the child's confidence in parents as sources of security and protection, even after controlling for the effects of parental sensitivity and warmth (also see Frosch et al., 2000). Similar questions can be raised about whether poor parenting practices predict insecurity in the context of interparental conflict as well as the parent-child relationship (Cummings & Davies, 2002; Grych, 1998). Given the paucity of research on this issue, no specific hypotheses are offered about the generality or specificity of associations between the parenting and interparental difficulties and insecurity in the two family relationships.

Another hypothesis, which we label the *outcome specificity hypothesis*, postulates that the magnitude of the paths between emotional security and children's developmental outcomes will vary as a function of the family context of security (i.e., interparental conflict versus parent-child attachment) and the form of maladjustment (i.e., internalizing versus externalizing symptoms), as illustrated by Paths 6 and 7 in Figure 6. Previous empirical tests of associations between child emotional security and child adjustment lend some support for this hypothesis. For example, Davies and Cummings (1998) reported that marital discord and children's emotional insecurity explains nearly three times more variance in internalizing symptoms than in externalizing symptoms. Likewise, other researchers have reported that internalizing symptoms are more consistently associated with indicators of insecurity in the interparental relationship than are externalizing symptoms (Davies et al., 2002; Harold & Shelton, 2000). Recent findings have also indicated that parent-child attachment security is more robustly associated with externalizing problems than internalizing symptoms in a model that also included measures of security in interparental conflicts (Harold & Shelton, 2000). Although these findings speculatively suggest that attachment security and security in the interparental conflicts may have different implications, the studies failed to test whether paths between the different types of security and forms of child maladjustment were significantly different from each other (Paths 6 and 7). Accordingly, the present study systematically tests for differences in the magnitude of these pathways.

In sum, this study is designed to examine the validity of both the direct effects and indirect effects hypotheses of emotional security. Guided by the direct effects hypothesis, emotional security in the interparental context is hypothesized to mediate the relationship between parental conflict and child adjustment even after taking into account the roles of parenting difficulties and parent-child attachment security. Consistent with the indirect effects hypothesis, parenting difficulties associated with parental conflict are hypothesized to increase the child's risk for adjustment problems through their association with child-parent attachment insecurity. Finally, we also examine whether associations between family factors, insecurity in family relationships, and child maladjustment differ significantly as a function of different forms of family difficulties (i.e., parental conflict, parenting difficulties), child insecurity (i.e., insecurity in the context of interparental conflict, child-parent attachment insecurity), and child maladjustment (i.e., internalizing, externalizing).

METHOD

Participants

Participants included 173 sixth- through eighth-grade students and their mothers from a public middle school in a working- and middle-class suburb bordering Rochester, New York. The participation rate among dyads of primary caregivers and children was 23%. Families were included in the present study if the mother and child (a) completed the study measures of interparental functioning, child emotional security, and child adjustment; (b) reported on the same interparental relationship as the child; and (c) maintained regular contact with the other parent at the time of the survey. Participating children were relatively evenly distributed across grade (57 sixth graders, 59 seventh graders, 57 eighth graders) and gender (91 girls, 82 boys). The mean age of the children was 12.58 years ($SD = 0.99$) and the largest proportion of them were White (92%), followed by smaller percentages of African Americans (4%), Native Americans (3%), and Hispanics (1%). Additional demographic data indicated that the sample was primarily middle- to lower-middle class. Median family income for this subsample exceeded $40,000 and the average number of years of completed education was 14.0 years for mothers and fathers ($SD = 2.25$ and 2.63, respectively). The majority of mothers were married or living with the father (87.3%), followed by small portions of divorced (8.1%) or separated (4.6%) families.

Procedure

Mailing lists with the addresses of students were provided to the principal investigator after school administrators gave their approval to the conduct of the study. Primary caregivers, who indicated an interest in participating in the study by returning a postcard in the mail, were sent survey forms on family and child functioning to complete and return in a postage-free envelope. Children who participated in the study completed their surveys on family and child functioning in their classrooms under the guidance of a trained experimenter. Participating children and mothers were entered into a lottery for a chance to win several gift certificates to local stores.

Measures

The goal of our overall measure was to obtain three manifest indicators for each of the key constructs in the model (e.g., interparental conflict, parenting, security measures, forms of child adjustment) as a way of forming stable, triangulated latent constructs without unnecessarily taxing the statistical model with additional parameter estimates (i.e., >3 indicators).

Interparental conflict. To assess destructive forms of interparental conflict, mothers completed the Verbal Aggression, Physical Aggression, and

Resolution scales of the Conflict and Problem-Solving Scales (CPS; Kerig, 1996). Scale items are rated on 4-point scales (0 = *never*, 3 = *often*), reflecting the frequency with which parents and their partners (a) engage in verbally aggressive conflict tactics such as yelling, accusing, and insulting (Verbal Aggression, 16 items; e.g., "Raise voice, yell, shout"; M = 24.46, SD = 8.28; range = 5–44); (b) exhibit physically aggressive conflict tactics, including threatening or inflicting physical harm (Physical Aggression, 14 items; e.g., "Push, pull, shove, grab partner"; M = 2.10, SD = 3.05; range = 0–18); and (c) resolve and manage disputes in a way that limits the proliferation of negativity and improves interparental relations (Resolution, 13 items; e.g., "We feel closer to each other than before the fight"; M = 3.77, SD = 13.70; range = –40–23). Internal consistency, test-retest reliability, and various forms of validity of the CPS are well-established (Kerig, 1996; 1998a). In the present sample, the CPS scales yielded adequate internal consistency (alphas ranged from .81 to .89).

Poor parenting practices. Mothers completed measures designed to assess three primary dimensions: parental acceptance, monitoring, and psychological control. First, an abbreviated version of the 20-item Acceptance scale of the Parental Acceptance and Rejection Questionnaire (PARQ) was used to assess maternal reports of her own (10 items) and her partner's (10 items) accepting and supportive behaviors with their child (Rohner, 1990). Sample items include "I [my partner] talk to my child in a warm and affectionate way" and "I [my partner] try to help my child when s/he is scared or upset." Parents responded to each statement by selecting one of four response options ranging from 1 = *almost always true* to 4 = *almost never true*. The aggregate measure, which subsumes standardized, maternal reports of mother and father acceptance (20 items), demonstrated good reliability in this sample (α = .89). The original PARQ Acceptance scale has good psychometric properties (Rohner, 1990).

Second, mothers reported separately on their own and their partner's monitoring on a scale commonly used in family research (e.g., Barber, 1996; Brown, Mounts, Lamborn, & Steinberg, 1993). Using a 4-point scale (1 = *don't know*, 4 = *know a lot*), mothers reported on their own and their partner's knowledge about the whereabouts of their child at night and school day afternoons (2 items each), how their child spends time (2 items each), and their child's friends (1 item each). Mothers' reports of their own and their partner's monitoring were standardized and summed to form a composite. The overall measure of parental monitoring evidenced good reliability in the present sample (α = .80).

Third, an adapted form of the Psychological Control Scale (PCS; Barber, 1996) was used to assess parental psychological control. Mothers reported on their own (8 items) and their partner's (8 items) use of psychological control or, more specifically, control strategies that negatively manipulate, discount, and limit children's psychological and emotional experiences. Sample items included "bring up my child's past mistakes when disciplining him/her," "would like to be able to tell my child how to feel or think about most things," and "avoid talking to my child when s/he hurts my feelings." Mothers rated how well each item characterized their own and their partners' parenting practices using a 4-point scale (1 = *not like me/my partner*, 4 = *a lot like me/my partner*). The original PCS, which was based on the Children's Report of Parental Behavior Inventory (Margolies & Weintraub, 1977), has demonstrated good reliability and psychometric properties. Mother reports of their own and their partner's use of psychological control were standardized and summed into a single measure. The alpha coefficient of the aggregate measure was .77.

Child emotional security in the context of interparental conflict. Child reactivity across the component processes of emotional security was assessed by child reports on the Security in the Interparental Subsystem Scale (Davies et al., 2002) and mother reports on an adapted measure of the Home Data Questionnaire—Adult Version (HDQ; Garcia O'Hearn et al., 1997). The following five SIS subscales were used in this study: (a) Emotional Reactivity, defined as multiple, prolonged, and dysregulated expressions of emotional distress (9 items; "When my parents argue, I feel scared," "When my parents argue, it ruins my whole day"); (b) Involvement, characterized by emotional and behavioral involvement in interparental conflicts (6 items; "When my parents have an argument, I try to comfort one or both of them"); (c) Avoidance, which reflects attempts to escape or avoid interparental conflict or its adverse aftermath (7 items; "When my parents have an argument, I feel like staying as far away from them as possible"); (d) Destructive Family Representations, which assesses appraisals of the deleterious consequences interparental conflict has for the welfare of the family (4 items; "When my parents have an argument, I wonder if they will divorce or separate"); and (e) Conflict Spillover Representations, defined as child expectancies that conflicts will spill over to affect their well-being and relations with parents (4 items; "When my parents have an argument, I feel like they are upset at me"). In addition to demonstrating adequate internal and test-retest reliability, support for the validity of these SIS subscales is shown by its links with measures of child reactivity to conflict, psychological problems, and exposure to parental conflict (Davies et al., in press). Alpha coefficients in the present sample were satisfactory, ranging from .71 to .87.

The original HDQ, which solicited parents' reports of the presence or absence of the child's specific reactions to conflict each day a conflict occurred, was modified in two ways. First, to increase the temporal period of assessments, we asked parents to rate how well each item described their child's reactions to witnessing interparental conflicts *over the past year* on a 5-point scale, ranging from 1 = *not at all like him/her* to 5 = *a whole lot like him/her.* Second, we developed additional items for the purpose of forming multi-indicator scales of security that were theoretically similar to the SIS subscales. The two scales used in this study were (a) *Emotional Reactivity*, which taps negative emotional arousal and dysregulation (5 items, e.g., "appears frightened," "still seems upset after we argue"; α = .76); and (b) *Involvement*, which reflects overt involvement and intervention in the arguments (5 items; α = .71; "tries to comfort one or both of us"). The validity of the revised HDQ is supported by its correspondence with child reports of similar forms of reactivity and its significance in larger profiles of child coping with interparental conflict (e.g., emotionality, involvement; see Davies et al., 2002).

Child and maternal reports of child conflict reactivity were subsequently standardized and summed into the three composites representing each of the component processes of security. The *emotional reactivity* composite consisted of parent and child reports on their respective Emotional Reactivity subscales; parental reports of Involvement and child reports of Involvement and Avoidance were indicators of the *regulation of conflict exposure* composite. The *internal representations* composite was comprised of child reports on the SIS Conflict Spillover and Destructive Family Representations subscales. The internal consistency of items comprising each of the composites was as follows: .86 for emotional reactivity, .76 for regulation of conflict exposure, and .86 for internal representations. Composites of emotional reactivity, regulation of conflict exposure, and internal representations were used as manifest indicators of a latent construct of emotional security in the context of interparental conflict.

Child-parent attachment security. Three scales were used to assess child attachment security in the parent-child relationship. First, given the paucity of self-report instruments designed to tap the child's emotionality, appraisals, and coping in parent-child relations, we developed a specific measure of security in the parent-child relationship that assesses emotional reactivity, regulation of exposure to parent affect, and internal representations. The majority of the 15 items on this scale were adapted from previous child report instruments designed to assess attachment security, including the Inventory of Parent and Peer Attachment (IPPA; Armsden & Greenberg, 1987), the Parental Attachment Questionnaire (PAQ; Kenny, Moilanen, Lomax, & Brabeck, 1993), the Security Scale (SS; Kerns, Klepac, & Cole, 1996), and the Relatedness Questionnaire (RQ; Lynch & Cicchetti, 1997). Evaluating attachment relations with mothers and fathers separately (a total of 30 items), children rated how well each statement described their emotional reactivity (e.g., "When I'm with this person, I feel better than I did before"), regulation of exposure to parents (e.g., "When I'm upset, I go to this person for comfort," "when I have a problem I can't solve, I go to this person for advice"), and internal representations (e.g., "I think this person is someone I can trust," "I think this person is a great parent") in their relations with their parents. Response alternatives ranged from 1 = *not at all true of me* to 4 = *very true of me*. Statements assessing insecurity were reverse scored so that higher values on the scale reflect greater security. Given their high intercorrelation, r (173) = .56, $p < .001$, child reports of mother and father attachment security were summed into a single composite of *child-parent attachment security* as a way of increasing scale reliability and the parsimony and power of the statistical models (α = .95 for the composite).

As another assessment of the child's internal representations of maternal and paternal emotional availability and support, children also completed an abbreviated version of the 20-item PARQ (Rohner, 1990). Children completed 10 items from the Child PARQ Acceptance Scale (e.g., "My mother [father] tries to help me when I am scared or upset," "My mother [father] cares about what I think and likes me to talk about it") to assess their appraisals of both mother and father availability. Response options ranged from 1 = *almost always true* to 4 = *almost never true*. Given the high correlation between maternal and paternal representations, r (173) = .70, $p < .001$, the two measures were summed to provide a parsimonious composite of negative *internal representations of parents* (α = .95 for the composite).

As another measure of the child's emotionality and regulation of exposure to parents in their attachment relations, mothers also completed a newly developed nine-item scale to assess parent-child attachment security. Mothers rated how well each statement described their child's relations with themselves and their partners on a 5-point scale, with response alternatives ranging from 1 = *not at all like my child* to 5 = *a whole lot like my child*. Sample items tapped the child's emotionality (e.g., "My child smiles and laughs with me [my partner]," "My child starts up pleasant conversations with me [my partner]") and ways of regulating relations with parents through secure-base behavior (e.g., "When my child is upset, he or she goes to me [my partner]," "My child appears comfortable sharing thoughts and feelings with me [my partner]"). Item development was heavily guided by earlier parent (e.g., Parent-Child Reunion Inventory; Marcus, 1997) and child report instruments of parent-child attachment security (e.g., SS; Kerns et al., 1996). Maternal reports of children's secure behaviors in the mother-child and father-child relationships were summed into a more parsimonious measure of *children's secure behavior* in light of their moderate to strong correspondence, r (173) = .58, $p < .001$. The internal consistency of the 18 items comprising the composite was $\alpha = .90$.

Child symptomatology. Children and parents completed the Anxious/ Depressed, Withdrawn, Delinquent, and Aggressive Behavior subscales from parallel forms of the Youth Self-Report and Child Behavior Checklist, respectively (Achenbach, 1991). The YSR and CBCL are widely used, well-validated measures of child adjustment problems (see Achenbach). Consistent with other constructs in the model, we reduced the number of indicators of internalizing and externalizing symptoms from four (2 child and 2 mother reports) to two by summing the child reports on (a) the Withdrawn and Anxious/Depressed scales into an internalizing symptoms measure, and (b) the Delinquency and Aggressive Behavior scales into an externalizing symptoms measure. Thus, internalizing symptoms were measured by maternal reports of Anxiety/Depression ($\alpha = .86$) and Withdrawal ($\alpha = .76$) and child reports of internalizing symptoms ($\alpha = .89$), whereas externalizing symptoms were measured by maternal reports of Aggression ($\alpha = .88$) and Delinquency ($\alpha = .65$) and child reports on the externalizing symptoms measure ($\alpha = .90$). This specific data reduction decision was guided by two rationales. First, assessments of the child's security in the parent-child and interparental relationships are based largely on child reports. Thus, placing heavier weight on parent reports in assessment batteries of child adjustment reduces informant variance in the statistical model and, as a result, provides a more conservative test of the mediational role of emotional security. Second, parents have a greater tendency to distinguish between forms of internalizing and externalizing symptoms than do children (Angold, Weissman, John, & Merikangas, 1987; Hay, Castle, & Davies, 2000). The relatively stronger correspondence across reports of different forms of maladjustment for child report increases systematic error variance and difficulties in obtaining a stable solution in structural equation models. Thus, we collapsed child reports into broadband maladjustment measures to increase the stability of the model.

RESULTS

Descriptive and Preliminary Analyses

Means, standard deviations, and correlations are presented in Table 5. Inspecting the correlations in the table provides a way of analyzing the utility of forming latent constructs for interparental conflict, parenting, insecurity in the interparental and parent-child relationships, and child internalizing and externalizing symptoms from multiple indicators. In support of the measurement model, intercorrelations among the indicators

72

TABLE 5

INTERCORRELATIONS AMONG INDICATORS OF INTERPARENTAL CONFLICT, PARENTING PRACTICES, CHILD INSECURITY IN THE CONTEXT OF INTERPARENTAL CONFLICT AND PARENT-CHILD ATTACHMENT RELATIONSHIPS, AND CHILD PSYCHOLOGICAL SYMPTOMS

Variables	1	2	3	4	5	6	7	8	9	10	11	12	13	14	15	16	17	M	SD
Marital conflict																			
1. Physical (P)	—																	2.10	3.04
2. Verbal (P)	.59	—																24.46	8.28
3. Resolution (P)	-.46	-.59	—															3.78	13.70
Parenting practices																			
4. Unsupportive (P)	.24	.34	-.38	—														0.00	0.79
5. Behavioral control (P)	-.22	-.30	.47	-.52	—													0.00	0.80
6. Psychological control (P)	.16	.43	-.42	.43	-.29	—												0.00	0.87
Child emotional insecurity																			
7. Emotional reactivity (A)	.30	.28	-.36	.14	-.14	.24	—											0.00	0.82
8. Regulation of exposure (A)	.23	.19	-.16	.00	.10	.21	.56	—										0.00	0.70
9. Internal representations (C)	.27	.31	-.28	.21	-.12	.26	.64	.52	—									0.00	0.88
Parent-child attachment insecurity																			
10. Child felt-security (C)	.14	.17	-.17	.23	-.28	.17	.13	-.07	.23	—								67.67	17.99
11. Secure behavior (P)	.18	.26	-.31	.45	-.43	.35	.14	.03	.19	.43	—							58.28	11.39
12. Internal representations (C)	.14	.16	-.11	.15	-.12	.06	.00	-.12	.20	.50	.29	—						32.05	12.26
Internalizing symptoms																			
13. Internalizing (C)	.06	.19	-.10	.12	-.20	.17	.45	.39	.56	.33	.14	.18	—					9.80	7.00
14. Anxiety/depression (P)	.18	.23	-.27	.24	-.20	.37	.45	.29	.36	.13	.38	-.40	.33	—				4.43	4.27
15. Withdrawn (P)	.14	.23	-.20	.31	.23	.30	.26	.09	.23	.22	.44	.20	.29	.65	—			2.47	2.59
Externalizing symptoms																			
16. Externalizing (C)	.20	.09	-.30	.16	-.14	.07	.19	.11	.39	.40	.22	.35	.51	.17	.12	—		11.86	8.55
17. Aggression (P)	.25	.22	-.12	.33	-.28	.33	.18	.13	.20	.10	.43	.20	.10	.58	.43	.31	—	7.19	5.81
18. Delinquency (P)	.24	.24	-.23	.28	-.29	.22	.20	.00	.29	.24	.42	.20	.11	.45	.42	.36	.65	1.39	1.84

Note.—P = parent-report measure; C = child-report measure; A = aggregate measure of child- and parent-reports.

of each of these constructs were moderate to strong: (a) interparental conflict, mean r (173) = .54; (b) parenting difficulties, mean r (173) = .41; (c) interparental insecurity, mean r (173) = .57; (d) parent-child insecurity, mean r (173) = .41; (e) internalizing symptoms, mean r (173) = .42; and (f) externalizing symptoms, mean r (173) = .44 (see the italicized correlations in Table 5).

Correlations among indicators of different latent variables also provide initial evidence for the proposed mediational paths in the family-wide model (see Table 5). Indicators of interparental conflict and parenting difficulties were, for the most part, significantly associated with measures of child internalizing and externalizing symptoms, thereby fulfilling the first condition necessary to demonstrate mediation (Baron & Kenny, 1986). Furthermore, results of preliminary structural equation models indicated significant direct paths running from interparental conflict to internalizing (β = .42, $p < .001$) and externalizing symptoms (β = .39, $p < .001$). Consistent with the second requirement that predictors should be associated with the proposed mediators, interparental conflict measures were, as a whole, associated with measures of parenting difficulties and children's insecurity in the context of interparental conflict. Likewise, assessments of parenting difficulties were associated with indices of parent-child security. Finally, the condition that the mediator be associated with the outcome variables was supported by consistent links among forms of child maladjustment and indicators of child insecurity in the context of interparental conflict and parent-child attachment relations.

Primary Analyses

Structural equation modeling with maximum likelihood estimation was used to test the family-wide model of emotional security. We first examined whether the partial mediational model (direct paths from interparental conflict and parenting difficulties to child internalizing and externalizing symptoms were included) provided a significantly better representation of the data than did the full mediational model (direct paths of interparental conflict and parenting difficulties are not specified). Adding the direct paths for interparental conflict and parenting difficulties did not result in a significant reduction in the chi-square ($\Delta\chi^2$ = 1.74, Δdf = 4, $p > .10$). Because these results indicate that the partial mediator model did not provide a significantly better representation of the data than did the full mediator model, the results of the more parsimonious, full mediator model are presented in Figure 7 (χ^2_{108} = 178.84, $p < .001$, GFI = .90, AGFI = .85, RMSEA = .06).

Consistent with our first hypothesis, which predicted direct effects, interparental conflict was significantly associated with insecurity in the

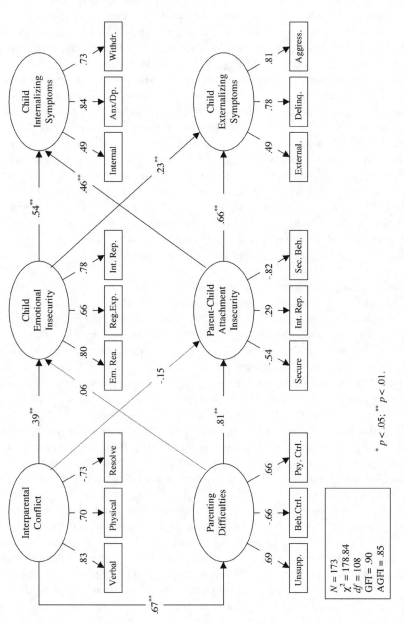

FIGURE 7.—A structural equation model testing the mediational role of child security in family relationships in the link between interparental conflict and parenting difficulties and child psychological symptoms.

N = 173
χ^2 = 178.84
df = 108
GFI = .90
AGFI = .85

$^*p < .05$; $^{**}p < .01$.

context of interparental conflict even after taking into account parenting difficulties. Child emotional insecurity, in turn, was significantly linked with internalizing and externalizing symptoms over and above the effects of parenting difficulties and parent-child attachment insecurity.

In accordance with our second hypothesis rooted in indirect effects models, interparental conflict was also indirectly linked with internalizing and externalizing symptoms through its associations with parenting difficulties and parent-child attachment insecurity. Specifically, parenting difficulties mediated the association between interparental conflict and attachment insecurity in the parent-child relationship. In turn, parent-child attachment insecurity mediated the link between parenting difficulties and the child's internalizing and externalizing symptoms.

In support of the specificity hypothesis, child insecurity in a particular family relationship was only related to the earlier experiential histories within that particular family relationship. Parental conflict was specifically associated with child insecurity in the context of interparental conflicts, but failed to be related to parent-child attachment insecurity. Similarly, parenting difficulties were unrelated to insecurity in the context of interparental conflict, but were associated with parent-child attachment insecurity.

To examine whether parental conflict was more strongly associated with insecurity in the context of interparental conflict than in the context of parenting difficulties, we compared the relative fit of the model in Figure 7, in which the paths among variables are free to vary (i.e., free-to-vary model), with the fit of a model in which the paths between (a) interparental conflict and insecurity in the interparental relationship and (b) parenting difficulties and insecurity in the interparental relationship are constrained to be equal (i.e., constrained model). Significant differences in the paths would be demonstrated if the free-to-vary model, which permits the paths to be different from each other, had a significantly lower chi-square statistic (i.e., better empirical fit) than the constrained model, which assumes the paths are equal to each other. The free-to-vary model did not provide a significantly better representation of the data than the constrained model, $\Delta\chi^2 = 0.05$, $\Delta df = 1$, $p > .80$, thereby indicating that parental conflict was not more strongly associated with insecurity in the context of interparental conflict than were parenting difficulties.

Similar model comparisons were conducted to examine whether parenting difficulties were more strongly associated with parent-child attachment insecurity than with interparental conflict. The free-to-vary model (i.e., model in Figure 7) yielded a significantly better fit to the data than did a model constraining to equivalence paths between (a) parenting difficulties and parent-child attachment insecurity, and (b) parental conflict and parent-child attachment insecurity, $\Delta\chi^2 = 25.79$, $\Delta df = 1$, $p > .001$.

Therefore, associations between parenting difficulties and parent-child attachment security were significantly stronger than associations between parental conflict and parent-child attachment security.

To examine whether associations between each form of insecurity and child internalizing and externalizing symptoms were significantly different in magnitude, four additional model comparisons were conducted. First, the free-to-vary model shown in Figure 7 was compared to a model in which path coefficients from parent-child attachment insecurity to internalizing and externalizing symptoms were constrained to be equal. The free-to-vary model yielded a significantly better fit to the model than did the constrained model, $\Delta\chi^2 = 6.71$, $\Delta df = 1$, $p = .01$, thereby indicating that parent-child attachment insecurity was more strongly associated with externalizing symptoms than with internalizing symptoms. Second, the free-to-vary model was compared to a model constraining path coefficients between insecurity in the context of interparental conflict and the two forms of psychological symptoms to equivalence. The free-to-vary model provided a marginally better representation of the data than did the constrained model, $\Delta\chi^2 = 3.51$, $\Delta df = 1$, $p = .06$. Thus, insecurity in the context of interparental conflict was more strongly associated with internalizing symptoms than with externalizing symptoms.

In the third set of model comparisons, the free-to-vary model did not yield a significantly better fit to the data than did a more parsimonious model that constrained to equivalence the path coefficients running from each type of insecurity (i.e., interparental conflict, attachment) to externalizing symptoms, $\Delta\chi^2 = 1.03$, $\Delta df = 1$, $p > .30$. Therefore, the results indicated that insecurity in the context of the interparental conflict and parent-child attachment insecurity were statistically comparable in their associations with externalizing symptoms. In the final set of comparisons, the free-to-vary model was compared to a model that constrained to equivalence the path coefficients running from each type of insecurity to internalizing symptoms. The free-to-vary model provided a significantly better representation of the data than did the constrained model, $\Delta\chi^2 = 7.83$, $\Delta df = 1$, $p < .01$. This finding indicated that insecurity in the context of interparental conflict was more strongly associated with internalizing symptoms than was parent-child attachment insecurity.

DISCUSSION

The overarching goal of this study was to extend the findings of Study 3 by examining whether interparental conflict may increase child vulnerability to adjustment problems through direct and indirect pathways. In the indirect pathway, parenting disturbances associated with interparental conflict were hypothesized to increase child adjustment problems by undermining child attachment security in the parent-child relationship. In support of this hypothesis, parenting difficulties characterized by lack of parental warmth, poor behavioral control, and high psychological control mediated the link between interparental conflict and parent-child attachment insecurity. These results are consistent with other recent studies reporting that dimensions of parenting mediate the link between marital conflict and child-parent attachment security (e.g., Frosch et al., 2000). However, the present results take the study of indirect pathways one step further by simultaneously demonstrating that insecurity in the parent-child attachment relationship is associated with child internalizing and externalizing symptoms. Thus, this study is the first to test and find support for a more comprehensive process model in which (a) parenting disturbances that accompany destructive interparental conflict are associated with greater insecurity in the parent-child relationship and (b) insecurity in the parent-child relationship, in turn, is linked with greater maladjustment even after specifying the effects of child insecurity in the face of interparental conflict (Cummings & Davies, 2002).

In the direct pathway, interparental conflict was hypothesized to affect child functioning by directly undermining the child's sense of security in the face of interparental conflict. In support of this hypothesis, child emotional insecurity remained a robust mediator of the link between interparental conflict and child internalizing and externalizing symptoms even after specifying the mediating effects of other family variables (i.e., parenting difficulties, parent-child attachment insecurity). Attesting to the robust nature of these direct pathways, the results also showed that (a) interparental conflict, but not parenting difficulties, is associated with child insecurity in the context of interparental conflict, and (b) child insecurity, in turn, is more strongly associated with internalizing symptoms than is parent-child insecurity. Thus, in the context of the emotional security hypothesis, these findings lend some support to the theoretical assumption that emotional security in the context of interparental conflict is a robust goal system that is distinct from parent-child insecurity in its developmental substance, correlates, and implications.

These findings also raise novel empirical concerns about the validity of strong versions of indirect effects models. In these models, parenting processes are conceptualized as fully mediating the association between interparental conflict and child maladjustment (e.g., Erel et al., 1998; Fauber et al., 1990; Fauber & Long, 1991; Mann & MacKenzie, 1996). The conclusions from studies of these models may be called into question because parenting processes are the only mechanisms included as mediators in tests of relations between parental conflict and child adjustment. To our knowledge, the present study is the only investigation to provide a more psychometrically fair test of direct effects by simultaneously incorporating direct effects mediators (i.e., child insecurity in the context of interparental conflict) with parenting mediators in the same model. The results, which support both direct and indirect pathways, indicate that parenting difficulties and parent-child attachment security are partial rather than full mediators of interparental conflict. In sum, the findings are more consistent with weak versions of indirect effects models and the emotional security hypothesis than with strong versions of indirect effects models.

Although the findings lend support to both direct and indirect pathways in our model, the strength of the mediational pathways varied as a function of the type of insecurity (i.e., interparental conflict, parent-child attachment) and form of child maladjustment (i.e., internalizing and externalizing symptoms). According to the outcome specificity hypothesis, the worry, vigilance, preoccupation, and involvement in interparental difficulties that reflect emotional insecurity are theorized to cohere into broader maladaptive coping patterns (e.g., learned helplessness, ruminative coping, self-blame) that are especially likely to increase child vulnerability to internalizing symptoms. In accordance with this hypothesis, the present findings indicate that child insecurity in the face of interparental conflict is more strongly linked with internalizing symptoms than with externalizing symptoms. Likewise, child insecurity in the context of interparental conflict is also more strongly associated with internalizing symptoms than with parent-child attachment insecurity. Additional comparisons of paths between parent-child attachment insecurity and the forms of child maladjustment indicated that attachment insecurity is more strongly associated with externalizing symptoms than with internalizing symptoms. Although these findings are consistent with some earlier findings (Harold & Shelton, 2000), additional research is needed to replicate results and explore the possible mechanisms that account for differential pathways between insecurity in different family relationships and various forms of child psychological maladjustment.

Another significant question addressed by this study is whether interparental conflict and parenting difficulties are risk factors that undermine child security within a specific family relationship or across multiple family relationships. Our findings specifically lend support to a predictor specificity hypothesis in demonstrating that (a) interparental conflict is the only factor associated with child insecurity in the face of parental conflict even when including parenting difficulties as independent variables in the analytic models, and (b) parenting is the only factor linked with parent-child attachment insecurity even when considering interparental conflict as an independent variable in the model. Moreover, the path between parenting practices and parent-child attachment insecurity is significantly stronger than the corresponding path between parental conflict and parent-child attachment insecurity. In the aggregate, these results suggest that child insecurity in a given family relationship may result largely from earlier histories within that specific relationship (Cummings & Davies, 1996; Davies & Cummings, 1994; Grych, 1998). However, other work has suggested that experiences in specific family relationships may predict security across multiple family relationships (see Cummings & Davies, 2002). For example, marital conflict has been shown to predict insecure parent-child attachment relationships even after statistically controlling for parental sensitivity and warmth (Frosch et al., 2000; Owen & Cox, 1997). Because a large part of the discrepancy in findings may be attributed to differences in parenting measures (e.g., our broad assessment of parenting versus more narrow assessments of parental availability in previous research), methodological designs (e.g., our mono-method design versus previous multi-method assessments), and sample characteristics (e.g., early adolescence versus early childhood samples), further delineating the specificity of these pathways remains an important direction for research.

V. STUDY 4: FAMILY CHARACTERISTICS AS POTENTIATING AND PROTECTIVE FACTORS IN THE ASSOCIATION BETWEEN PARENTAL CONFLICT AND CHILD FUNCTIONING

Although the results of the previous studies provide considerable support for the association between destructive forms of parental conflict and children's difficulties in functioning, the modest to moderate magnitude of these linkages suggests that there is considerable heterogeneity in the outcomes of children exposed to similar levels of conflict. Why do children who are exposed to similar histories of parental conflict cope and adapt to conflict in different ways? Consistent with calls for a second generation of research on interparental conflict (Cummings & Cummings, 1988; Fincham, 1994), the aim of this study is to explicate the contextual characteristics that are associated with the amplification or dampening (i.e., moderators) of associations between interparental conflict and child functioning. Guided by our goal of embedding the study of interparental processes in the larger family system, our specific aim is to identify the family processes that moderate the link between interparental conflict and child functioning. Because both the emotional security hypothesis and social learning theory offer clear, but differing, predictions about the nature of these moderating effects, this study specifically examines whether the nature of the interplay between interparental conflict and these family processes supports one or both of these theories.

According to the emotional security hypothesis, family processes may be associated with the strengthening or weakening associations between (a) interparental conflict and child insecurity in the context of interparental conflict, and (b) child insecurity and child internalizing and externalizing symptoms. Family characteristics are conceptualized as protective or potentiating factors in three different domains of the family system. Specifically, the magnitude of associations between parental conflict, emotional insecurity, and child adjustment are hypothesized to vary as a function of (a) broad family-level factors characterized by family cohesion and instability, (b) more specific interparental relationship characteristics reflected in emotional expressiveness and relationship satisfaction, and (c) parent-child processes evidenced by child-parent attachment insecurity and parenting difficulties (i.e., psychological control, poor monitoring, low warmth).

Guided by our conceptualization in Chapter I, we specifically hypothesize that family cohesion, interparental relationship satisfaction, and interparental emotional expressiveness will act as protective factors in associations between parental conflict, insecurity in the context of interparental conflict, and child maladjustment. Interparental conflict is hypothesized to take on a different, more benign meaning in the context of warm, cohesive, and expressive family relationships. In particular, the confluence of these factors may signify that any unresolved hostility is unlikely to disrupt warm, stable relationships among family members. Furthermore, interparental conflict is also hypothesized to be less threatening to the child if it is simply part of a larger tendency for parents to express both positive and negative affect. Thus, because the conflicts occur in the context of warm, well-regulated family relationships, children from these homes have no sound basis for being concerned about the impact conflicts may have on the welfare of themselves or their family (Davies & Cummings, 1994). The derivative hypothesis is that the relationship between interparental conflict and child emotional insecurity will be weaker for children who experience warm, cohesive, and expressive family relationships.

These same family characteristics are also hypothesized to serve as protective factors in associations between child insecurity and psychological maladjustment. Access to emotional support, comfort, and protection within warm family relationships may provide important resources that allow the child to successfully cope with and manage worries and insecurities about family difficulties. As a result, these factors may serve to weaken or offset the ill effects of emotional insecurity for children's long-term adjustment.

In contrast, any signs of broader family vulnerabilities characterized by family instability, parenting difficulties, and child-parent attachment insecurity are hypothesized to potentiate or magnify associations between parental conflict, child insecurity in the interparental context, and child maladjustment. The emotional security hypothesis proposes that the child should be particularly concerned about preserving security when interparental conflict is part of a broader family context characterized by distress, instability, and adult psychological vulnerability. Interparental conflict and hostility in these families may be more likely to proliferate to disrupt family functioning and threaten the well-being of the child (e.g., increase the likelihood of spillover of hostility into parent-child relations). Thus, the primary hypothesis is that parental conflict is especially likely to be associated with child insecurity in interparental contexts when they also co-occur with family instability, parenting difficulties, and child-parent attachment insecurity.

The emotional security hypothesis also proposes that the child's specific worries and insecurities about the interparental relationship are more likely to intensify and spread into other family and personal domains if they take place in the face of other family vulnerabilities. Worries, distress, and coping difficulties, which may otherwise be successfully contained within interparental contexts, are more likely to become increasingly prominent experiences in discordant homes. The spread and intensification of worries may eventually develop into internalizing and externalizing symptoms that are stable across time and context. Thus, insecurity in the context of interparental conflict is hypothesized to be most strongly associated with psychological symptoms when the child is also experiencing high levels of family instability, parenting difficulties, and insecure parent-child attachment relationships.

Consistent with the emotional security hypothesis, social learning theory proposes that the magnitude of associations between destructive parental conflict and child functioning depends, in part, on the quality of the child's relationships with the parents. However, social learning theory differs from the emotional security hypothesis in its specific focus on the relationship between interparental conflict and child aggressive and antisocial behaviors. In further contrast to the emotional security hypothesis, social learning theory proposes that the greatest risk for emulating the aggression and hostility in interparental conflicts occurs when the child more readily identifies with parents. Thus, within social learning theory, it is hypothesized that the relationship between interparental conflict and child aggression will actually be more pronounced when the child experiences warm, secure relationships with parents (i.e., parent-child security, warm parenting, family cohesion). In contrast, the emotional security hypothesis predicts the opposite pattern: Interparental conflict is expected to be more strongly associated with behavioral dysregulation when family relationships are insecure and lacking in cohesiveness and warmth.

METHOD

Participants and Procedure

Participants in this study were the 173 parent-child dyads who participated in Study 3 (see the Method section of Chapter IV for details). The survey packets completed by mothers and children also contained mother surveys assessing family moderators and mother and child surveys of child aggressive behavior.

Measures

To maintain comparability between Study 3 and 4, our primary goal was to utilize the Study 3 assessments of interparental conflict, parenting difficulties, parent-child attachment insecurity, child emotional insecurity, and psychological symptoms. However, because regression analyses are the preferred statistical model for examining the moderating effects of continuous variables (Holmbeck, 1997), it was not possible to use these measures as manifest indicators of latent constructs in SEM. Thus, the proposed manifest indicators of each of the latent variables in Study 4 were standardized and summed to form more reliable, parsimonious composites. The composites and their respective standardized indicators were as follows: (a) *interparental conflict*, the sum of maternal report measures on the CPS Verbal Aggression, Physical Aggression, and Resolution (reverse scored) scales (Kerig, 1996); (b) *parenting difficulties*, the sum of maternal reports of parental behavioral control (reverse scored), psychological control, and low warmth; (c) the *child's emotional insecurity in the context of interparental conflict*, the sum of three composite variables used to assess emotional reactivity (mother and child reports), regulation of conflict exposure (mother and child reports), and internal representations; (d) *parent-child attachment insecurity*, the sum of measures indexing children's appraisals of low parental warmth, child reports of parent-child attachment security (reverse scored), and maternal reports of parent-child attachment security (reverse scored); (e) *child internalizing symptoms*, the sum of child reports of internalizing symptoms from the YSR and mother reports of Anxious/Depressed and Withdrawn behavior from the CBCL; and (f) *child externalizing symptoms*, the sum of maternal reports on the CBCL Delinquent and Aggressive Behavior scales and child reports of externalizing symptoms from the YSR.

Child behavioral dysregulation. The child externalizing symptoms composite, which was specified as an outcome measure in tests of the social learning theory hypotheses, was supplemented with two additional measures of the child's behavioral dysregulation in response to parental conflicts. First, children provided reports of their behavioral dysregulation on the Behavioral Dysregulation subscale of the Security in the Interparental Subsystem scale. The three items comprising the scale were designed to assess dysregulated, hostile behaviors in response to interparental conflicts (e.g., "When my parents have an argument, I yell at, or say unkind things, to people in my family," "When my parents have an argument, I hit, kick, slap, or throw things at people in my family"). The alpha coefficient for the subscale in this sample was satisfactory ($\alpha = .68$). Second, mothers also reported on the child's overt signs of reactivity to conflict using the Behavioral Dysregulation subscale from the revised version of the Home Data Questionnaire—Adult Version (Davies et al., 2002; Garcia O'Hearn et al., 1997). The Behavioral Dysregulation subscale of the HDQ-AV consists of three items that very closely correspond to the child reports on the SIS Behavioral Dysregulation subscale (e.g., the extent to which the child's reactions to witnessing parental arguments is characterized as "starts yelling at or saying unkind things to family members," "starts hitting, kicking, slapping, or throwing things at family members"). Reliability for the scale in this sample was adequate (α = .64). Given that child and mother reports on their respective measures of behavioral dysregulation were moderately correlated, r (173) = .52, $p < .001$, the two measures were standardized and summed together to form a parsimonious, multi-informant, composite of behavioral dysregulation.

Family moderators. Four additional maternal report measures were employed to more comprehensively examine various family characteristics as moderators of the mediational pathways. First, *family cohesion* was assessed by mother reports on the Family Cohesion Scale of the Family Adaptability and Cohesion Evaluation Scales–III. The FACES-III Family Cohesion scale contains 10 items designed to assess family bonding and support (e.g., "Family members feel very close to each other"), with response options ranging from 1 = *almost never* to 5 = *almost always*. The Family Cohesion scale has been shown to have adequate reliability (α = .86) and support for validity has been reflected in its ability to discriminate between clinic and nonclinic families (Olson, Portner, & Lavee, 1985) and predict family and child functioning in theoretically meaningful ways (Davies & Windle, 1997).

Second, *family instability*, which is defined as the degree to which families fail to provide continuity, cohesiveness, and stability for children, was measured using a revised version of the Family Instability Index (FII; Ackerman, Kogos, Youngstrom, Schoff, & Izard, 1999). Consistent with this index, the current measure consists of nine items tapping the number of times the family experienced disruptive life events over the past five years in five family domains: (a) changes in residence, (b) changes in the primary and/or secondary caregiver, (c) transitions in romantic relationships of the primary caregiver (e.g., dissolution, new romantic relationships, initiation of cohabitation), (d) job and income loss, and (e) death or serious illness of a close family member (M = 2.90, SD = 2.56, range = 0–12). Parental stressful life events, which were indicators of the original family instability measure, were not included in the current assessment because they were "events that may have happened to the caregiver" (Ackerman et al., 1999; p. 260), such as a close friend of the caregiver moved away or the caregiver experienced occupational stressors; they do not definitively capture family-level events that directly disrupt the continuity of children's lives (i.e., the source of disruption lies outside of the family). The validity of the original and revised versions of the FII has been demonstrated by its hypothesized associations with other family characteristics and children's coping and psychological adjustment (Ackerman et al., 1999; Forman & Davies, in press).

Third, *interparental relationship satisfaction* was assessed by mother reports on the Relationship Assessment Scale (RAS; Hendrick, 1988). The RAS contains seven items designed to assess spousal or partner satisfaction (e.g., "In general, how satisfied are you with your relationship?"). Mothers rated each item on a 5-point Likert scale. The RAS has adequate reliability, and support for its validity is evidenced by its associations with assessments of love, commitment, investment, and satisfaction (Hendrick, 1988). Alpha in the present sample was .96.

Fourth, mothers completed the Leveling subscale from the Managing Affect and Differences Scale (MADS; Arellano & Markman, 1995) to assess *interparental emotional expressiveness.* The eleven items on the MADS Leveling scale are designed to assess the clarity, simplicity, and constructiveness of interparental discussions of feelings, thoughts, and difficulties (e.g., "When my partner is upset by something I have done, s/he tells me," "I say exactly what I think or feel," "I offer constructive alternatives for his/her bothersome behavior"). Response options range from 1 = *strongly disagree* to 5 = *strongly agree.* In addition to demonstrating excellent reliability (α = .90 in this sample), the validity of the Leveling scale is reflected in its significant relations with relationship satisfaction, problem intensity, and efficacy (Arellano & Markman, 1995).

RESULTS

Descriptive and Preliminary Analyses

The means, standard deviations, and intercorrelations for the primary variables are presented in Table 6. The correlations among the variables provided preliminary data for examining the utility of the moderator models. First, evaluating whether the family characteristics protect or potentiate children's vulnerability to parental conflict and insecurity requires demonstrating that the proposed risk factors (i.e., parental conflict, child insecurity) predict children's vulnerability. Supporting this criterion and the findings from Study 4, the results indicated that interparental conflict was significantly associated with child insecurity (r (173) = .30). Child insecurity, in turn, was related to child internalizing and externalizing symptoms (mean r (173) = .41). Second, the modest collinearity between the proposed risk factors and the proposed family moderators underscores the

TABLE 6

ASSOCIATIONS AMONG PARENTAL CONFLICT, INTERPARENTAL SECURITY, CHILD SYMPTOMS, AND THE PROPOSED FAMILY MODERATORS

Variables	1	2	3	4	5	6	7	8	9	10	M	SD
1. Parental conflict	—										0.00	2.15
2. Child emotional insecurity	.30*	—									0.00	2.03
3. Child internalizing symptoms	.22*	.52*	—								0.00	2.35
4. Child externalizing symptoms	.21*	.29*	.52*	—							0.00	2.37
5. Child behavioral dysregulation	.29*	.35*	.34*	.72*	—						0.00	1.74
6. Family cohesion	-.36*	-.22*	-.26*	-.38*	-.28*	—					40.77	5.49
7. Family instability	.05	.10	.12	.14	.05	-.01	—				2.90	2.56
8. Interparental expressiveness	-.21*	-.17*	-.21*	-.17*	-.14*	.44*	.02	—			39.01	7.45
9. Interparental satisfaction	-.42*	-.30*	-.17*	-.20*	-.29*	.44*	-.17*	.50*	—		28.53	6.51
10. Parent-child insecurity	.24*	.14	.33*	.43*	.29*	-.37*	.13	-.26*	-.27*	—	0.00	2.33
11. Parenting difficulties	.33*	.23*	.35*	.38*	.30*	-.47*	.11	-.32*	-.49*	.41*	0.00	2.34

Note.—*$p < .05$.

potential viability of the moderator model, mean $r(173) = .23$. Third, our decision to retain each of the family characteristics as distinct variables in the moderator analyses was supported by the modest to moderate intercorrelations among the proposed family moderator variables, mean $r(173) = .29$. Finally, given the relatively high correlation between the child's internalizing and externalizing symptoms ($r(173) = .52$), it is possible that forming a single, aggregate measure of psychological maladjustment might provide a more parsimonious account of the data. Preliminary analyses for tests of the emotional security hypothesis indicated that the pattern of moderating effects was similar across models of internalizing and externalizing symptoms. Accordingly, we standardized and summed the two outcome measures into a single composite of psychological maladjustment for tests of emotional security predictions ($M = 0.00$, $SD = 4.11$). However, given the significance of hostility and aggression in social learning accounts, child externalizing symptomatology was retained as a distinct variable in tests of social learning theory.

To examine whether the predictor and moderator effects differed significantly for boys and girls, gender was specified as a predictor and moderator in the regression models. The findings indicated that gender failed to moderate the main effects of the predictors (i.e., parental conflict, child insecurity) or the Predictor × Moderator interaction terms. Moreover, including gender as a covariate (i.e., main effect) did not change the nature of the interactions between parental conflict and the proposed family moderators. Therefore, gender was dropped from primary analyses to increase the parsimony, statistical power, and generalizability of the findings.

Primary Analyses Plan

Hierarchical multiple regression models were conducted to examine the moderating role of family characteristics in links between interparental conflict, child reactivity to conflict, and child maladjustment. The first two subsections of the results test predictions made by the emotional security hypothesis. The first examines whether the association between interparental conflict and the child's insecurity in the context of interparental conflict is moderated by each of the six family characteristics; the second subsection examines interactions between child insecurity and each of the six family moderators in predicting child psychological maladjustment. To test predictions derived from social learning theory, the final subsection examines the moderating role of warm, involved, and cohesive parent-child relationships in the link between parental conflict and the child aggressive behavior.

Following recommendations in earlier research (e.g., Curran & Chassin, 1996), separate regression analyses were specified for the combination of each moderator (i.e., six family characteristics) and predictor to increase the power to detect moderator effects, reduce problems with multicollinearity, and retain the distinct nature of each family factor. Consistent with guidelines for testing moderator models (Baron & Kenny, 1986; Holmbeck, 1997), the main effects of the predictor and proposed moderators were entered first in the regression followed by the two-way interaction between the predictor and moderator. This hierarchical procedure specifically examines whether the interaction predicts significant variance in the outcome variable after statistically controlling for the main effects of the predictor and moderator. Given that the main effects of the predictors in the regression models are highly comparable to the correlational findings in Table 6 and the SEM results in Study 4, only the results of the interaction terms are reported for the sake of parsimony. Significant interactions were clarified by plotting regression slopes at high (1 SD) and low (−1 SD) levels of the moderator. Post hoc statistical tests were also conducted to examine whether the regression slopes representing associations between the predictor and outcome were significantly different from 0 at high (1 SD) and low (−1 SD) levels of the moderator.

Family Moderators in the Link Between Parental Conflict and Child Insecurity

Six hierarchical multiple regression models were conducted to examine the interplay between the predictor (i.e., parental conflict) and each of the six proposed moderators in predicting child insecurity.

Family-level characteristics. Although family cohesion failed to moderate the link between parental conflict and child insecurity, the Parental Conflict × Family Instability interaction was significantly associated with child emotional insecurity, $F(1, 169) = 4.56$, $p < .05$, $r^2 = .024$. Plots of the regression slopes showed that associations between parental conflict and child emotional insecurity were particularly strong in the context of relatively high levels of family instability. Post hoc statistical tests indicated that interparental conflict was linked with child insecurity at both higher, $\beta = .19$, $p < .005$, and lower, $\beta = .12$, $p < .05$, levels of family instability.

Interparental relationship characteristics. Separate regression analyses indicated that the child's sense of security was predicted by a Parental Conflict × Interparental Expressiveness interaction, $F(1, 169) = 10.10$, $p < .005$, $r^2 = .051$, and a Parental Conflict × Interparental Relationship Satisfaction interaction, $F(1, 169) = 5.03$, $p < .05$, $r^2 = .025$. Plots of the regression slopes showed that the link between parental conflict and child emotional

89

insecurity is weakest when mothers report high levels of interparental emotional expressiveness and relationship satisfaction. Simple slope analyses further revealed that parental conflict was associated with emotional insecurity at (a) lower, $\beta = .25$, $p < .001$, and higher, $\beta = .13$, $p < .05$, levels of interparental emotional expressiveness and (b) lower, $\beta = .19$, $p < .01$, but not higher, $\beta = .06$, $p > .20$, levels of interparental relationship satisfaction.

Parent-child characteristics. Parenting difficulties and parent-child attachment insecurity failed to moderate the association between parental conflict and child emotional insecurity in the context of interparental conflict.

Family Moderators in the Link Between Child Emotional Insecurity and Symptoms

Six hierarchical multiple regression analyses were also conducted to assess the interaction between child insecurity in the interparental relationship and each of the six family moderators in predicting child psychological symptoms.

Family-level characteristics. Although family instability failed to moderate the effects of the child's emotional insecurity, the Family Cohesiveness × Child Insecurity interaction significantly predicted child maladjustment, $F(1, 169) = 7.10$, $p < .01$, $r^2 = .029$. Plots of the regression lines indicated that the child's emotional insecurity was more weakly associated with their maladjustment when they experienced higher levels of family cohesion. Simple slope analyses indicated that the relation between child insecurity and child maladjustment was significant at higher, $\beta = .25$, $p < .01$, and lower, $\beta = .51$, $p < .001$, levels of family cohesion.

Interparental relationship characteristics. Child maladjustment was significantly predicted by the Interparental Expressiveness × Child Insecurity interaction, $F(1, 169) = 6.50$, $p < .01$, $r^2 = .028$, and the Interparental Satisfaction × Child Insecurity interaction, $F(1, 169) = 4.66$, $p < .05$, $r^2 = .021$. In plotting the regression slopes, the association between the child's insecurity and child maladjustment was demonstrated to be the weakest when mothers reported high levels of interparental emotional expressiveness and relationship satisfaction. Post hoc statistical tests further revealed that the child's insecurity was significantly associated with psychological symptoms at both low and high levels of (a) interparental emotional expressiveness ($\beta = .52$, $p < .001$; $\beta = .29$, $p < .005$, respectively) and (b) interparental relationship satisfaction ($\beta = .53$, $p < .001$; $\beta = .27$, $p = .01$, respectively).

90

Parent-child characteristics. The association between the child's insecurity and the child's psychological maladjustment was moderated by parent-child attachment insecurity, $F(1, 169) = 7.20$, $p < .01$, $r^2 = .026$, and parenting difficulties, $F(1, 169) = 5.90$, $p < .025$, $r^2 = .023$. Graphical plots indicated that relations between the child's emotional insecurity and psychological maladjustment were strongest in the context of high levels of parent-child attachment insecurity and greater parenting difficulties. Results of the simple slope analyses indicated that the association between child insecurity and child maladjustment was significant at both high and low levels of (a) parent-child attachment insecurity ($\beta = .50$, $p < .001$; $\beta = .23$, $p < .05$, respectively) and (b) parenting difficulties ($\beta = .50$, $p < .001$; $\beta = .24$, $p < .05$, respectively).

Social Learning Theory Moderators in the Link Between Parental Conflict and Child Aggression

Six hierarchical multiple regression analyses were specified to examine the moderating role of the three family characteristics (i.e., parenting practices, parent-child attachment security, and family cohesion) in the relationship between parental conflict and two aggression measures (i.e., child behavioral dysregulation in response to conflicts, externalizing symptoms).

Parenting. Parenting practices (i.e., composite of warmth, behavioral control, and psychological control) moderated the relationship between parental conflict and child behavioral dysregulation, $F(1, 169) = 4.81$, $p < .05$, $r^2 = .030$, and externalizing symptoms, $F(1, 169) = 3.85$, $p = .05$, $r^2 = .019$. However, counter to predictions derived from social learning theory, simple slope analyses indicated that interparental conflict was associated with child behavioral dysregulation in the context of high ($\beta = .40$, $p < .001$) but not low ($\beta = .05$, *ns*) levels of parenting difficulties. Similarly, the relationship between parental conflict and child externalizing symptoms was significant at high ($\beta = .26$, $p < .05$) rather than low ($\beta = -.04$, *ns*) levels of parenting difficulties.

Child-parent attachment security. The Parental Conflict × Parent-Child Attachment Insecurity interaction was associated with child behavioral dysregulation, $F(1, 169) = 5.98$, $p < .05$, $r^2 = .030$, and externalizing symptoms, $F(1, 169) = 3.61$, $p < .06$, $r^2 = .017$. However, follow-up tests revealed that associations between interparental conflict and child behavioral dysregulation and externalizing symptoms were only significant when parent-child attachment insecurity was high, $\beta = .37$, $p < .001$ and $\beta = .22$, $p = .01$, respectively. Conversely, when children experienced relatively low levels of parent-child attachment insecurity, associations between parental conflict and the child's behavioral dysregulation ($\beta = -01$, *ns*) and externalizing symptoms ($\beta = -.06$, *ns*) were not significant.

Family cohesion. Although family cohesion failed to moderate the link between parental conflict and child externalizing symptoms, $F(1, 169) = 1.02$, $p > .30$, the interaction between family cohesion and parental conflict was significantly associated with behavioral dysregulation, $F(1, 169) = 5.06$, $p < .05$, $r^2 = .026$. Counter to social learning theory hypotheses, simple slope analyses indicated that parental conflict was associated with child behavioral dysregulation at low ($\beta = .26$, $p = .001$) rather than high ($\beta = -.03$, *ns*) levels of family cohesion.

DISCUSSION

Although the results of Studies 2 and 3 lend consistent support to the hypothesis that child response processes account for the association between interparental conflict and the child psychological symptoms (Davies & Cummings, 1998), the moderate magnitude of these pathways suggests that there is considerable variability in the role child response processes play in models of family and child risk. Both the emotional security hypothesis and social learning theory propose that this variability stems from differences in child histories of exposure to other family characteristics. In these models, family characteristics are cast as moderators of relationships between interparental and child functioning. However, each theory makes contrasting predictions about the nature of the moderating role of family characteristics. According to the emotional security hypothesis, family difficulties and stressors potentiate or magnify associations between interparental conflict, child reactivity to conflict, and child adjustment, whereas family harmony and warmth may buffer or weaken these associations. Conversely, social learning theory proposes that associations between interparental conflict and child aggressive responding are actually more pronounced when parent-child relationships are characterized by high levels of warmth, cohesiveness, and security. The overall pattern of findings indicated that family characteristics moderated the relations between interparental conflict and child functioning in the direction hypothesized by the emotional security hypothesis.

Family characteristics were specifically shown to moderate the links between (a) interparental conflict and the child insecurity in the interparental relationship and (b) child insecurity and the child's psychological symptoms. According to the emotional security hypothesis, family characteristics served as either potentiating or protective factors in models of interparental conflict and child insecurity. Forms of family adversity characterized by family instability, parenting difficulties, and parent-child attachment insecurity were expected to potentiate or exacerbate the concerns of children from high-conflict homes because they signify that parental conflict is occurring in the context of a fragile family system. Thus, these forms of family adversity may further prime the heightened vigilance, distress, and hostile appraisals of the children who have been exposed to high levels of conflict. Although adversity in the parent-child relationship (i.e., parenting difficulties, parent-child insecurity) failed to moderate the effects of interparental conflict, the association between interparental conflict and emotional insecurity did vary as a function of family instability. In partial support of the potentiating hypothesis, interparental conflict is more strongly linked with child emotional insecurity when a child experiences high levels of family instability.

Conversely, family factors that reflect cohesiveness and harmony in the family system were hypothesized to protect the child from the stress associated with parental conflict. Consistent with this hypothesis, the results indicate that interparental relationship satisfaction and expressiveness are protective factors in the link between parental conflict and child insecurity. Parental conflict was a particularly weak predictor of insecurity for children whose parents reported high levels of satisfaction and a tendency to directly, simply, and constructively discuss thoughts and feelings in their relationship. According to the emotional security hypothesis, when heightened destructive conflict occurs in the presence of a broader, cohesive relationship between parents, it may signify to children that the deleterious effects of conflict have minimal or negligible implications for the welfare of the family or themselves. Consequently, conflict may pose less of a threat to child emotional security in these contexts.

Our findings further indicated that the implications emotional insecurity has for the child's psychological maladjustment may also depend on family characteristics. Interestingly, although parenting difficulties and parent-child attachment insecurity were not potentiating factors in the first link in the mediational chain, these factors did have potentiating effects on associations between the child's emotional insecurity and child maladjustment. Although child insecurity was significantly related to child adjustment problems across different levels of parent-child difficulties, the association between parental insecurity and child maladjustment was especially pronounced when a child experienced high levels of parenting difficulties and parent-child insecurity. In accord with Path 7 in Figure 1, these findings suggest that the high levels of child emotional insecurity may be more apt to proliferate and crystallize into broader patterns of psychological difficulties when a child is also faced with significant stressors in the parent-child relationship.

By the same token, family factors characterized by adult cohesiveness, satisfaction, and expressiveness in the interparental relationship actually protect insecure children from developing psychological problems. Similar to the pattern of findings with potentiating factors, child emotional insecurity was significantly associated with psychological problems at both high and low levels of the three family protective factors. However, pathways between child insecurity and psychological maladjustment were significantly weaker when a child experienced relatively high levels of family cohesiveness, parental satisfaction, and interparental expressiveness. When interpreted in the emotional security hypothesis, one explanation for these findings is that children who experience high levels of insecurity may still gain confidence in the ability of the family unit to serve as base of protection and security if they have access to other family resources and strengths. The broader sense of security procured from these other family resources may offset some of the vulnerability of the child who experiences high levels of insecurity in the context of interparental conflict.

The results yielded weak to modest empirical support for hypotheses articulated in social learning theory. Consistent with social learning theory, the correlations between interparental conflict and child behavioral dysregulation and externalizing symptoms were significant and modest to moderate in magnitude. When interpreted in the context of social learning theory, these findings are consistent with the notion that the child may develop conduct problems by modeling the hostile, aggressive behaviors displayed by parents during bouts of conflict. However, several other theories make very similar predictions about associations between parental conflict and child conduct problems. Thus, multiple alternative explanations exist for these findings. For example, to the extent that forms of behavioral dysregulation (e.g., hitting) can be viewed as signifying emotional dysregulation or a defensive stance against interpersonal threat, behavioral dysregulation can be interpreted conceptually as a key dimension of emotional insecurity (Davies et al., 2002). Within family systems theory, elevated disruptive behaviors of children from high conflict homes may serve to distract parents from their serious interparental difficulties as they unite to address child symptoms (Cox & Paley, 1997; Emery, 1989; Margolin et al., 2001). Genetic transmission theories also propose that links between parental conflict and child conduct problems are mediated, in part, by genes (e.g., antisocial personality; Margolin et al., 2001).

Additional questions can be raised about the distinct moderator hypotheses derived from social learning theory. Social learning theory postulates that warm, secure parent-child and family relationships should be associated with the amplification of the relationship between interparental conflict and child aggression. However, moderator analyses yielded an opposite pattern of findings: Associations between interparental conflict and child hostile behaviors were significantly stronger at low rather than at high levels of parent-child warmth, attachment security, and family cohesiveness. Thus, there was no evidence for the hypothesis that a child is more likely to model parents' hostility in the context of warm parent-child and family relationships. Rather, consistent with the potentiating hypothesis within the emotional security model, difficulties in family relationships appear to amplify associations between interparental conflict and child disruptive functioning.

The findings, though they provide support for the emotional security hypothesis, do not necessarily discount the importance of social learning theory or conceptual explanations articulated in other theories. Our goal was to test the validity of different predictions about the nature of moderating effects of family characteristics described in social learning theory and the emotional security hypothesis. Thus, this study was designed to examine only a small component of each of these theories. There are also other plausible, alternative explanations for the findings. Although the mediational pathways in emotional security hypothesis cast family variables as moderators of the association between emotional insecurity and child maladjustment, other conceptualizations might dissect and interpret the interactions in different ways. For example, child emotional insecurity could be examined as a moderator of the link between family instability and child maladjustment. Organism-environment models in developmental psychopathology provide a particularly plausible alternative explanation for these results. The environmental component within these models is reflected in the set of family variables (e.g., family instability, cohesiveness), whereas the organism component consists of child insecurity in the context of interparental conflict (Margolin & Gordis, 2000; Wachs, 1991; Windle & Tubman, 1999). Likewise, research inspired by the cognitive-contextual framework has examined contextual factors such as parenting practices as moderators in associations between interparental conflict and child responses to conflict (Grych, 1998).

Consistent with the emotional security hypothesis, the primary message of this study is that family difficulties potentiate pathways among interparental conflict history, child emotional insecurity, and child maladjustment. Conversely, the findings showed that indicators of supportive family relationships are protective factors that appear to weaken or dilute pathways among parental conflict, insecurity, and child maladjustment.

VI. CONCLUSIONS, IMPLICATIONS, AND FUTURE DIRECTIONS

The results of this *Monograph*, as a whole, support a complex, process-oriented explanation for associations between interparental conflict and child coping and adjustment. In particular, evidence was found for various aspects of the process-oriented explanation derived from the emotional security hypotheses (see Figure 1). The data are also consistent with other process models for the relationship between interparental conflict and the child's functioning. Notably, findings partly support the importance of the cognitive-contextual framework (i.e., perceived threat, self-blame). Moreover, outcomes are consistent with an indirect effects model for parenting processes as partially, but not fully, mediating the effects of interparental conflict.

In comparing and contrasting effects of imitation and modeling versus emotional security, Study 1 provided evidence more consistent with the emotional security hypothesis. The results of that study, described in Chapter II, thus are consistent with the first link in the mediational chain for the emotional security hypothesis (Path 1 in Figure 1). Interpretation in terms of social learning mechanisms was qualified by the infrequent incidence of precise imitation or the modeling of the same-gender parent. Moreover, counter to a social learning model, the findings of Study 4, described in Chapter V, indicate that children are not more likely to model parental aggression as a function of parental warmth or other positive aspects of parent-child relationships. Furthermore, the more general modeling response of heightened behavioral dysregulation would also be predicted as a function of the emotional reactivity component of the emotional security hypothesis as well as by other major theories in this area (e.g., Crockenberg & Langrock, 2001a; Grych & Fincham, 1990). It was also the case that other aspects of the data would not be predicted by the social learning model. For example, the much higher prevalence of regulatory than dysregulatory responses, the greater association of increased parental aggression with fear than anger, and the importance of emotional security themes in the topics of interparental conflict to the child's responding all raise questions about the operation of some social learning mechanisms in models of interparental conflict. Thus, although various alternative explanations may explain why the data were not consistent with social learning theory (e.g., children may have learned responses but not performed them in these particular testing contexts), the results of Studies 1 and 4, on balance, suggest that this model provides a substantially more limited explanation than the emotional security hypothesis.

Moreover, other recent work has extended the utility of the emotional security hypothesis for accounting for the effects of exposure to forms of interparental conflict on the child. For example, Goeke-Morey, Cummings, Harold, and Shelton (2002) have shown, based on analogue research designs testing the child's reactions to a wide range of marital conflict tactics, that the effects of exposure to interparental conflict depend on how interparental conflicts are expressed and the nature of the topics of conflicts. Moreover, in a particularly important extension of the study of forms of conflict, their work supports the notion that forms of interparental conflict can be either constructive or destructive, with orderings of conflict behaviors along broad continua of relative constructiveness and destructiveness made possible by scoring the child's responding based on the components of emotional security (i.e., emotional reactivity, internal representations, regulation of exposure to parental conflict). For example, based on the emotional security hypothesis, Goeke-Morey and colleagues (2002) postulated that forms of interparental conflict should be classified as constructive if they are associated with more positive than negative emotional responses from the child. In fact, quite a number of behaviors *occurring in the context of interparental conflicts* met these criteria (e.g., support). Thus, conceptual and measurement bases for advancing the study of the parameters of interparental conflict were derived from the emotional security hypothesis, including the novel proposition that the child's exposure to some forms of conflict may pose no threat to emotional security or possibly may even enhance it, as suggested by the high rate of positive emotional responding to conflict strategies.

This message is a hopeful one, given that everyday conflicts are surely inevitable in close relationships. A next step is to test these propositions in the context of predicting the child's long-term functioning (Figure 1, Paths 1–4), optimally in the context of prospective longitudinal research (Cummings, Davies, & Campbell, 2000). Research on interparental conflict and the child's functioning has almost always focused on the prediction of adjustment problems. However, it follows from the findings regarding constructive conflict that the construct of Child Psychological Maladjustment in Figure 1 should be broadened to include measures pertinent to possible positive outcomes (e.g., increased social skills, secure attachment relationships) as well as adjustment problems.

Like any reasonably well-articulated conceptual framework, the model for this *Monograph* also serves to highlight various remaining gaps in knowledge that await future research. Returning to Figure 1, it can be seen that the effects of forms of interparental conflict on family characteristics (Path 5) and the reciprocal effects of family characteristics on forms of interparental conflict (Path 6) are prominent conceptual pathways in this model. Accordingly, it will be important to examine the indirect (see Paths 5–7 in Figure 1) as well as direct effects of various forms of constructive and destructive interparental conflict.

Moreover, returning to the construct of Interparental Conflict in the figure, it will be interesting to investigate if forms of interparental conflict can be described in terms of higher order interparental conflict styles as well as specific conflict strategies. For example, can several distinctive styles of destructive or constructive conflict be identified (Katz & Gottman, 1993; Katz & Wooden, 2002)? Given the identification of higher order styles, it is important to determine how these styles relate to particular strategies for expressing interparental conflict. Taking matters a step further, one might examine the interplay between these different levels of analysis (macro and micro) in predicting child functioning and adjustment. For example, how does the child respond to particular forms of conflict expression in the context of particular interparental conflict styles?

Finally, from a methodological perspective, it will be important to determine if results addressing the child's reactions to interparental conflict correspond across analogue, survey, observational, and other methods of collecting data. Every method has strengths and weaknesses. Thus, it is always important to study phenomenon over time with different methodologies. If similar, or converging, effects are obtained across methods, confidence in findings is increased. For example, Cummings, Goeke-Morey, and Dukewich (2001) have advocated the use of parental diaries to study the child's reactions to exposure to forms of interparental conflict in the home, with parents carefully trained to code interparental conflict and the child's reactions in the home. It will be interesting to see if future studies employing diary methodologies provide support for effects of exposure to interparental conflict behaviors based on analogue methodologies.

The process-oriented explanation provided by the emotional security hypothesis hinges importantly on a particular conceptualization of mediating and indirect effects (Davies & Cummings, 1994, 1998). Without support for the predictions of the emotional security hypothesis regarding mediational processes associated with exposure to marital conflict (Paths 1–4 in Figure 1), the completeness, as well as uniqueness, of the process-oriented account is limited. Moreover, it is important to compare and contrast the explanation provided against alternative mediational models. In Study 2, we compared the mediational models provided by the emotional security hypothesis and the cognitive contextual framework. Notably, in the context of Figure 1, Study 2 provides evidence suggestive of links between interparental conflict and child emotional security (Path 1); interrelations between the three component processes, as reflected in loadings of manifest indicators on the latent construct of emotional security (Path 3); and associations between emotional security and child maladjustment (Path 4). In addition, evidence is provided by Study 2 that emotional security processes fare well in relation to the explanatory model provided by the cognitive contextual framework. That is, the pathway between interparental conflict and emotional security processes is relatively robust in comparison to the pathways between interparental conflict and cognitive-contextual processes. Similarly, the pathway between emotional security processes and child adjustment is relatively robust in comparison to the pathways between cognitive-contextual processes and child adjustment. The specific implications of the comparisons of these two major models for the effects of exposure to marital conflict were discussed at some length above.

A particular strength of the present results testing the mediational role of components of emotional security in relation to past reports is that these tests were based on longitudinal data. Prospective designs permit a more precise articulation of relationships among family processes and child coping and adjustment. Currently, most work pertaining to effects of conflict histories is based on correlations (or the equivalent) between questionnaire instruments of conflict history and child reactions or adjustment (Fincham & Grych, 2001; Margolin et al., 2001). Nonetheless, a gap that needs to be addressed in future research is to test these propositions in the context of multiwave (three or more), prospective, longitudinal research. Stronger inferences about developmental pathways can be gained from tests including three or more time points of assessment. That is, effects related to age, passage of time, and the characteristics of change across development periods can be better understood and articulated when child and family functioning is prospectively observed over multiple time points (Cummings et al., 2000).

Study 2 tested a model for the emotional security hypothesis based on a latent construct of emotional security. It is also of interest to test pathways through each of the components of emotional security (see Figure 1). In this regard, Harold, Shelton, Goeke-Morey, and Cummings (2001) recently focused on these issues by examining the mediational role of the three component processes of emotional security in associations between interparental conflict and child adjustment. The findings were consistent with the notion that each of the components of emotional security contributed to pathways between interparental conflict and child adjustment, largely replicating and extending results previously reported by Davies and Cummings (1998) (Paths 2 and 3 in Figure 1).

A gap in model testing reflected in much past research on interparental conflict and child functioning is the narrow focus on either the direct effects of exposure to marital conflict or the indirect effects of marital conflict through its association with parenting. Clearly, there are considerable bases for expecting that both direct and indirect effects of parenting are prominent pathways in predicting the child's functioning (Buchanan & Heiges, 2001; Cox, Paley, & Harter, 2001; Krishnakumar & Buehler, 2000). This *Monograph* attempted to simultaneously address both directions of explanation through the utilization of multiple programmatic studies centered around a common model (see Paths 1–7 in Figure 1). Studies 1 and 2 focused on in-depth tests of questions about direct effects pathways (Paths 1–4); Studies 3 and 4 examined direct and indirect effects in the same analyses (Paths 1–7). A notable strength of the last two studies reported in the *Monograph* is full representation of direct and indirect pathways, including processes that mediate effects.

Few studies have examined the effects of interparental conflict from a family-wide perspective addressing (a) direct effects of interparental relationships, (b) indirect effects of interparental conflict through parent-child relationships, and (c) the impact of family factors beyond those associated with exposure to interparental conflict. To remedy this gap, Studies 3 and 4 addressed these issues from a family-wide perspective. Study 3 presents a fully articulated comparison of direct and indirect effects models. Consistent with the theory (Cummings & Davies, 1996), both direct (Paths 1 and 4) and indirect (Path 5) pathways emerged as predictors of child adjustment. This study is among the first to fully represent the direct effects pathways in family-wide tests by including assessments of mediational processes associated with exposure in model testing rather than only global assessments of exposure to interparental conflict. The finding that both direct and indirect pathways independently contribute to the prediction of child outcomes in this context is noteworthy. The results are especially noteworthy in supporting the main predictions from the emotional security hypothesis and predictions made by other researchers (e.g., Frosch et al., 2000; Owen & Cox, 1997). The findings specifically support the hypothesis that emotional security is affected by the qualities of both the interparental and parent-child relationships. Moreover, in demonstrating that emotional security in the parent-child and the interparental relationships are each mediators in the prediction of child adjustment problems, the results highlight the potential of studying the dynamics of emotional security in the broader family system.

100

The results of Study 3 also suggest that the characteristics and correlates of insecurity in the parent-child and interparental relationships may be relatively distinct. Thus, interparental insecurity was most robustly linked with child internalizing symptomatology, but insecurity in the parent-child relationship was more closely associated with child externalizing symptoms. Moreover, in models that simultaneously incorporated interparental conflict and parenting, interparental conflict history was the only factor associated with insecurity in the context of interparental conflict. Conversely, parenting was the only factor associated with attachment insecurity in parent-child relationships. These findings suggest that in high-conflict homes child adjustment problems may result from the operation of several different pathways of influence arising from marital discord. For example, child emotional problems may be most closely tied to broader concerns about family functioning, safety, and stability arising from repeated exposure to interparental conflict, whereas child conduct problems in these homes may be primarily linked with problems in parenting associated with elevated interparental conflict. In summary, support emerged for a family-wide model of the relationship between interparental conflict and child adjustment via exposure to interparental conflict and parenting difficulties, with indications that direct and indirect pathways may be relatively independent in terms of the nature of the mechanisms underlying child adjustment.

Given that this *Monograph* outlines a new direction for fully articulated family-wide models for interparental conflict, emotional security about family relationships, and child functioning, it will be interesting to see whether future studies replicate these initial tests. A limitation with regard to the assessment strategy in the present work is that observationally based measures of attachment were not used and might well be expected to be more closely related to interparental conflict than are the present assessments. Thus, the mediational role of parenting in associations between interparental conflict and children's internalizing symptoms and the direct pathways between interparental conflict and attachment security may be more likely to emerge from an assessment scheme that focuses on more traditional and data-intensive measures of this specific construct of parent-child attachment (Owen & Cox, 1997).

Moreover, Study 3 focused primarily on understanding child negative outcomes. A promising direction for future research is to examine links between constructive interparental conflict, the child's increased security in multiple family systems, and positive child development outcomes (Paths 1–7 in Figure 1). Other family systems beyond the interparental and parent-child systems may also play important roles in associations between interparental conflict and child functioning. Accordingly, another direction for future research is to examine the influence of interparental conflict on the child in association with additional family systems (Paths 5–7). For example, assessment of sibling relationships may advance models of interparental conflict and child functioning (Dunn & Davies, 2001).

Although research has focused on how child reactions to interparental conflict change as a function of variations in forms of interparental conflict (e.g., Study 1 in this *Monograph*), the model for this *Monograph* (illustrated in Figure 1) proposes that variations in other aspects of family functioning may also be associated with child responding (Paths 6 and 7). The study of how contextual factors or characteristics may moderate responding to family processes is a relative gap in family research. In particular, few studies have considered how other family factors might affect or moderate the impact of interparental conflict. For example, adopting a developmental psychopathology perspective (Cummings et al., 2000), one might expect that protective or buffering factors outside the context of marital dispute would diminish associations between interparental conflict and the child's emotional security (Path 6) and adjustment (Path 7), whereas vulnerability or potentiating factors beyond the context of interparental discord would exacerbate the vulnerability of the child faced with high levels of interparental conflict (Paths 6 and 7).

Study 4 demonstrated the moderating role of other family characteristics in pathways between interparental conflict and child functioning. The fact that interparental relationship satisfaction and expressiveness reduce the magnitude of the association between interparental conflict and child emotional security (Path 6) makes considerable sense when one considers that child emotional security is theorized to hinge on the meaning interparental functioning has for the welfare of the family and child. For some families, interparental conflict may be more of a stylistic way of communicating rather than a clean expression of animosity and hostility toward the other individual. Interparental relationship satisfaction and expressiveness convey a message to the child that may offset the message otherwise inherent in interparental conflict. Thus, the broader pattern of relationship functioning may convey to the child that the parents hold each other in high regard despite their relatively unvarnished method of communicating negative thoughts and feelings.

The potentiating and protective aspects of family characteristics were both evident in associations between emotional security in the context of interparental conflict and child psychological adjustment (Path 7). Although interparental insecurity consistently predicted child psychological adjustment, regardless of the other family characteristics, family factors were still associated with the size or magnitude of relations between security and adjustment. The message of these results again is that the child evaluates the larger picture concerning family relationships in assessing its meaning for the self and family. At the same time, interparental conflict emerged as a risk factor for child adjustment, despite the nature of any broader conditions in the family. A future direction in advancing a more complete family-wide model of interparental conflict is to examine other family factors and their potential role in moderating pathways among interparental conflict and the child's functioning. Among the other factors that hold promise as potentially significant factors are parental depression (Cummings & Davies, 1999), divorce (Buchanan & Heiges, 2001), and single-parent and stepfamilies (Fine, 2001). Testing the moderating role of family factors within prospective designs is also an important research direction in light of the possibility that these results are due, in large part, to the child affecting the interparental relationship and other aspects of family functioning.

In conclusion, this *Monograph* yielded findings pertinent to a process-oriented understanding of the relationship between interparental conflict and child functioning by testing processes and pathways proposed in the emotional security hypothesis in the context of alternative models of interparental conflict. The emotional security hypothesis fared well in relation to tests against alternative hypotheses. However, it has never been the claim that this model provides more than one of several midlevel process explanations for effects. Consistent with this assumption, evidence was found for the importance of other processes (Cummings et al., 2000). Moreover, it is anticipated that evidence for the significance of additional goals in guiding the child's responses to interparental and family functioning will be found in future studies (Crockenberg & Langrock, 2001a, 2001b).

Furthermore, various other theoretical propositions are possible. For example, Margolin et al. (2001) have called attention to the variety of possible classes of theoretical perspectives on interparental conflict and child adjustment, including family systems theory, social learning theory, spillover hypotheses, genetic transmission theories, and trauma theory. Notably, elements of several of these broad theoretical directions about relations of interparental conflict and child functioning are to some extent subsumed within the four conceptual views tested in the current *Monograph*. For example, both the emotional security hypothesis and the cognitive contextual model make propositions pertinent to family processes (i.e., emotional security, perceptions of threat), spillover hypotheses (i.e., indirect effects propositions), and trauma theory (i.e., sensitization). However, other notions are not tested by theories described in this report (e.g., genetic transmission) and various other directions within these classes of theories could be considered. For example, coercive process models, which constitute a class of social learning theories, propose that links between interparental conflict and child functioning may be explained, in part, by behavioral contingencies in behaviors parents display toward children. Misbehavior displayed by the child during bouts of interparental conflict may specifically be negatively reinforced when parents end aversive interactions with each other to discipline the child (e.g., Emery, 1989) or when parents, in their preoccupation with their ongoing dispute, respond to the misbehavior by acting in a positive or neutral manner to escape aversive parent-child conflicts (Patterson, 1982; Patterson, Capaldi, & Bank, 1991). In either case, the child's misbehavior serves as a stimulus for ending aversive stimuli (e.g., parent-child or interparental conflicts) and is thus strengthened or intensified through negative reinforcement (Cummings & Davies, 1994). Moreover, empirical directions regarding the possible significance of interparental conflict to relationships with other individuals, such as siblings (Dunn & Davies, 2001) or peers (Parke et al., 2001), merit further consideration. Thus, the present report was limited to tests of several of the most currently influential theoretical approaches, with especially well-developed conceptual and empirical foundations. However, a variety of other directions toward the fuller articulation of empirical models and testing of alternative theories might be pursued in the future.

Notably, this interlocking series of conceptual and empirical studies pertinent to the emotional security hypothesis advanced a common set of programmatic themes as reflected in Figure 1. Strengths of this package of reports with regard to testing of the cogency of the emotional security hypotheses and comparisons with alternative theories include reliance on multiple methodologies, samples, and cultures to investigate overlapping themes that are supported by a common model. Moreover, as we have also shown, this model points the way to broader directions in future research, as implicated by the current findings as well as by gaps left unattended in the model outlined in Figure 1. It is thus hoped that this *Monograph* provides some inspiration for taking the next steps toward advancing understanding of these significant family relationships from a process-oriented perspective, including the consideration and testing of advanced process models of associations between interparental conflict and child adjustment in the context of family-wide, prospective longitudinal research designs (e.g., Cummings & Davies, 2002; Grych & Fincham, 2001; Harold et al., 1997).

REFERENCES

Achenbach, T. M. (1991). *Integrative guide for the 1991 CBCL / 4–18, YSR, and TRF profiles.* Burlington, VT: University of Vermont, Department of Psychiatry.

Ackerman, B. P., Kogos, J., Youngstrom, E. A., Schoff, K., & Izard, C. E. (1999). Family instability and the problem behaviors of children from economically disadvantaged families. *Developmental Psychology, 35,* 258–268.

Ainsworth, M. D. S., Blehar, M. C., Waters, E., & Wall, S. (1978). *Patterns of attachment: A psychological study of the strange situation.* Hillsdale, NJ: Lawrence Erlbaum.

Andrews, J. A., Hops, H., & Duncan, S. C. (1997). Adolescent modeling of parent substance use: The moderating effect of the relationship with the parent. *Journal of Family Psychology, 11,* 259–270.

Angold, A., Weissman, M., John, K., & Merikangas, K. (1987). Parent and child reports of depressive symptoms in children at low and high risk for depression. *Journal of Child Psychology and Psychiatry, 28,* 901–915.

Arellano, C. M., & Markman, H. J. (1995). The Managing Affect and Differences Scale (MADS): A self-report measure assessing conflict management in couples. *Journal of Family Psychology, 9,* 319–334.

Armsden, G. C., & Greenberg, M. T. (1987). The Inventory of Parent and Peer Attachment: Individual differences and their relationship to psychological well-being in adolescence. *Journal of Youth & Adolescence, 16,* 427–454.

Bandura, A. (1973). *Aggression: A social learning analysis.* Englewood Cliffs, NJ: Prentice-Hall.

Bandura, A. (1983). Psychological mechanisms of aggression. In R. G. Geen & E. I. Donnerstein (Eds.), *Aggression: Theoretical and empirical reviews* (Vol. 1). New York: Academic Press.

Bandura, A., & Walters, R. H. (1959). *Adolescent aggression.* New York: Ronald.

Barber, B. K. (1996). Parental psychological control: Revisiting a neglected construct. *Child Development, 67,* 3296–3319.

Baron, R. M., & Kenny, D. A. (1986). The moderator-mediator variable distinction in social psychological research: Conceptual, strategic, and statistical considerations. *Journal of Personality and Social Psychology, 51,* 1173–1182.

Belsky, J., & Cassidy, J. (1994). Attachment: Theory and evidence. In M. Rutter, D. Hay, & S. Baron-Cohen (Eds.), *Develomental principles and clinical issues in psychology and psychiatry* (pp. 373–402). Oxford, UK: Blackwell.

Blatz, W. E. (1966). *Human security: Some reflections.* Toronto: University of Toronto Press.

Block, J. H., Block, J., & Morrison, A. (1981). Parental agreement-disagreement on childrearing orientations and gender-related personality correlates in children. *Child Development, 52,* 965–974.

Bollen, K. A. (1989). *Structural equations with latent variables.* New York: Wiley.

Bowlby, J. (1969). *Attachment and loss. Vol. I: Attachment.* New York: Basic Books.

Bretherton, I., Ridgeway, D., & Cassidy, J. (1990). Assessing internal working models of the attachment relationship. In M. T. Greenberg, D. Cicchetti, & E. M. Cummings (Eds.), *Attachment in the preschool years: Theory, research, and intervention.* Chicago: University of Chicago Press.

Brown, B. B., Mounts, N., Lamborn, S. D., & Steinberg, L. (1993). Parenting practices and peer group affiliation in adolescence. *Child Development, 64,* 467–482.

Buchanan, C. M., & Heiges, K. L. (2001). When conflict continues after the marriage ends: Effects of post-divorce conflict on children. In J. Grych & F. Fincham (Eds.), *Child development and interparental conflict.* New York: Cambridge University Press.

Buss, A., & Durkee, A. (1957). An inventory for assessing different kids of hostility. *Journal of Consulting Psychology, 21,* 343–349.

Cassidy, J., Parke, R. D., Butkovsky, L., & Braungart, J. M. (1992). Family-peer connections: The roles of emotional expressiveness within the family and children's understanding of emotions. *Child Development, 63,* 603–618.

Christensen, A., & Margolin, G. (1988). Conflict and alliance in distressed and non-distressed families. In R. A. Hinde & J. Stevenson-Hinde (Eds.), *Relationships within families: Mutual influences.* New York: Oxford University Press.

Colin, V. L. (1996). *Human attachment.* New York: McGraw-Hill.

Cox, M. J., & Paley, B. (1997). Families as systems. *Annual Review of Psychology, 48,* 243–267.

Cox, M. J., Paley, B., & Harter, K. (2001). Interparental conflict and parent-child relationships. In J. Grych & F. Fincham (Eds.), *Child development and interparental conflict.* New York: Cambridge University Press.

Crockenberg, S. B., & Covey, S. L. (1991). Marital conflict and externalizing behavior in children. In D. Cicchetti & S. Toth (Eds.), *Rochester Symposium on Developmental Psychopathology: Vol. 3. Research and clinical contributions to a theory of developmental psychopathology.* Rochester, NY: University of Rochester Press.

Crockenberg, S. B., & Forgays, D. (1996). The role of emotion in children's understanding and emotional reactions to marital conflict. *Merrill-Palmer Quarterly, 42,* 22–47.

Crockenberg, S. B., & Langrock, A. (2001a). The role of emotion and emotion regulation in children's responses to interparental conflict. In J. Grych & F. Fincham (Eds.), *Child development and interparental conflict.* New York: Cambridge University Press.

Crockenberg, S., & Langrock, A. (2001b). The role of specific emotions in children's responses to interparental conflict: A test of the model. *Journal of Family Psychology, 15,* 163–182.

Cummings, E. M. (1998). Children exposed to marital conflict and violence: Conceptual and theoretical directions. In G. Holden, B. Geffner, & E. Jouriles (Eds.), *Children exposed to marital violence: Theory, research, and applied issues.* Washington, DC: American Psychological Association.

Cummings, E. M., & Cicchetti, D. (1990). Towards a transactional model of relations between attachment and depression. In M. Greenberg, D. Cicchetti, & E. M. Cummings (Eds.), *Attachment in the preschool years: Theory, research, and intervention.* Chicago: University of Chicago Press.

Cummings, E. M., & Cummings, J. S. (1988). A process-oriented approach to children's coping with adults' angry behavior. *Developmental Review, 3,* 296–321.

Cummings, E. M., & Davies, P. T. (1994). *Children and marital conflict: The impact of family dispute and resolution.* New York: Guilford.

Cummings, E. M., & Davies, P. T. (1995). The impact of parents on their children: An emotional security hypothesis. *Annals of Child Development, 10,* 167–208.

Cummings, E. M., & Davies, P. T. (1996). Emotional security as a regulatory process in normal development and the development of psychopathology. *Development and Psychopathology, 8,* 123–139.

Cummings, E. M., & Davies, P. T. (1999). Depressed parents and family functioning: Interpersonal effects and children's functioning and development. In T. Joiner & J. C. Coyne (Eds.), *The interactional nature of depression: Advances in interpersonal approaches.* Washington, DC: American Psychological Association.

Cummings, E. M., & Davies, P. T. (2002). Effects of marital conflict on children: Recent advances and emerging themes in process-oriented research. *Journal of Child Psychology and Psychiatry,* **43**, 31–63.

Cummings, E. M., Davies, P. T., & Campbell, S. B. (2000). *Developmental psychopathology and family process: Theory, research, and clinical implications.* New York: Guilford.

Cummings, E. M., Davies, P., & Simpson, K. (1994). Marital conflict, gender, and children's appraisal and coping efficacy as mediators of child adjustment. *Journal of Family Psychology,* **8**, 141–149.

Cummings, E. M., Goeke-Morey, M. C., & Dukewich, T. L. (2001). The study of relations between marital conflict and child adjustment: Challenges and new directions for methodology. In J. H. Grych & F. D. Fincham (Eds.), *Child development and interparental conflict.* New York: Cambridge University Press.

Cummings, E. M., Goeke-Morey, M. C., Papp, L. M., & Dukewich, T. L. (in press). Children's responses to mothers' and fathers' emotional behavior and conflict tactics during marital conflict in the home. *Journal of Family Psychology.*

Cummings, E. M., Hennessy, K., Rabideau, G., & Cicchetti, D. (1994). Responses of physically abused boys to interadult anger involving their mothers. *Development and Psychopathology,* **6**, 31–41.

Cummings, E. M., Vogel, D., Cummings, J. S., & El-Sheikh, M. (1989). Children's responses to different forms of conflict expression of anger between adults. *Child Development,* **60**, 1392–1404.

Cummings, E. M., Zahn-Waxler, C., & Radke-Yarrow, M. (1981). Young children's responses to expressions of anger and affection by others in the family. *Child Development,* **52**, 1274–1282.

Cummings, J. S., Pellegrini, D., Notarius, C., & Cummings, E. M. (1989). Children's responses to angry adult behavior as a function of marital distress and history of interparental hostility. *Child Development,* **60**, 1035–1043.

Curran, P. J., & Chassin, L. (1996). A longitudinal study of parenting as a protective factor for children of alcoholics. *Journal of Studies on Alcohol,* **57**, 305–313.

Dadds, M. R., Atkinson, E., Turner, C., Blums, G. J., & Lendich, B. (1999). Family conflict and child adjustment: Evidence for the cognitive-contextual model of intergenerational transmission. *Journal of Family Psychology,* **13**, 194–208.

Davies, P. T., & Cummings, E. M. (1994). Marital conflict and child adjustment: An emotional security hypothesis. *Psychological Bulletin,* **116**, 387–411.

Davies, P. T., & Cummings, E. M. (1995). Children's emotions as organizers of their reaction to interadult anger: A functionalist perspective. *Developmental Psychology,* **31**, 677–684.

Davies, P. T., & Cummings, E. M. (1998). Exploring children's emotional security as a mediator of the link between marital relations and child adjustment. *Child Development,* **69**, 124–139.

Davies, P. T., Forman, E. M., Rasi, J. A., & Stevens, K. I. (2002). Assessing children's emotional security in the interparental subsystem: The Security in the Interparental Subsystem (SIS) scales. *Child Development,* **73**, 544–562.

Davies, P. T., & Lindsay, L. (2001). Does gender moderate the effects of conflict on children? In J. Grych & F. Fincham (Eds.), *Child development and interparental conflict.* New York: Cambridge University Press.

Davies, P. T., Myers, R. L., Cummings, E. M., & Heindel, S. (1999). Adult conflict history and children's subsequent responses to conflict. *Journal of Family Psychology*, **13**, 610–628.

Davies, P. T., & Windle, M. (1997). Gender-specific pathways between maternal depressive symptoms, family discord, and adolescent adjustment. *Developmental Psychology*, **33**, 657–668.

Davies, P. T., & Windle, M. (2001). Interparental discord and adolescent adjustment trajectories: The potentiating and protective role of intrapersonal attributes. *Child Development*, **72**, 1163–1178.

Davis, B. T., Hops, H., Alpert, A., & Sheeber, L. (1998). Child responses to parental conflict and their effects on adjustment: A study of triadic relations. *Journal of Family Psychology*, **12**, 163–177.

Dunn, J., Brown, J., & Beardsall, L. (1991). Family talk about feeling states and children's later understanding of others' emotions. *Developmental Psychology*, **27**, 448–455.

Dunn, J., & Davies, L. (2001). Sibling relationships and interparental conflict. In J. Grych & F. Fincham (Eds.), *Child development and interparental conflict*. New York: Cambridge University Press.

El-Sheikh, M. (1997). Children's response to adult-adult and mother-child arguments: The role of parental marital conflict and distress. *Journal of Family Psychology*, **11**, 165–175.

El-Sheikh, M., Cummings, E. M., & Reiter, S. (1996). Preschoolers' responses to interadult conflict: The role of experimentally manipulated exposure to resolved and unresolved arguments. *Journal of Abnormal Child Psychology*, **24**, 655–679.

El-Sheikh, M., & Flanagan, E. (2001). Parental problem drinking and children's adjustment: Family conflict and parental depression as mediators and moderators of risk. *Journal of Abnormal Child Psychology*, **29**, 417–432.

Emery, R. E. (1982). Interparental conflict and the children of discord and divorce. *Psychological Bulletin*, **92**, 310–330.

Emery, R. E. (1989). Family violence. *American Psychologist*, **44**, 321–328.

Emery, R. E., Fincham, F. D., & Cummings, E. M. (1992). Parenting in context: Systemic thinking about parental conflict and its influence on children. *Journal of Consulting and Clinical Psychology*, **60**, 909–912.

Emery, R. E., & O'Leary, K. D. (1982). Children's perceptions of marital discord and behavior problems of boys and girls. *Journal of Abnormal Child Psychology*, **10**, 11–24.

Erel, O. & Burman, B. (1995). Interrelatedness of marital relations and parent-child relations: A meta-analytic review. *Psychological Bulletin*, **118**, 108–132.

Erel, O., Margolin, G., & John, R. S. (1998). Observed sibling interactions: Links with the marital and the mother-child relationship. *Developmental Psychology*, **34**, 288–298.

Fauber, R. E., Forehand, R., Thomas, A. M., & Wierson, M. (1990). A mediational model of the impact of marital conflict on adolescent adjustment in intact and divorced families: The role of disrupted parenting. *Child Development*, **61**, 1112–1123.

Fauber, R. L., & Long, N. (1991). Children in context: The role of the family in child psychotherapy. *Journal of Consulting and Clinical Psychology*, **59**, 813–820.

Fincham, F. D. (1994). Understanding the association between marital conflict and child adjustment: An overview. *Journal of Family Psychology*, **8**, 123–127.

Fincham, F. D., Beach, S. R. H., Harold, G. T., & Osborne, L. N. (1997). Marital satisfaction and depression: Different causal relationships for men and women? *Psychological Science*, **8**, 351–357.

Fincham, F. D., & Grych, J. H. (2001). Advancing understanding of the association between interparental conflict and child development. In J. Grych & F. Fincham (Eds.), *Child development and interparental conflict*. New York: Cambridge University Press.

Fincham, F. D., Grych, J. H., & Osborne, L. N. (1994). Does marital conflict cause child maladjustment? Directions and challenges for longitudinal research. *Journal of Family Psychology*, **8**, 128–140.

Fine, M. A. (2001). Marital conflict in stepfamilies. In J. H. Grych & F. Fincham (Eds.), *Child Development and Interparental Conflict*. New York: Cambridge University Press.

Forman, E. M., & Davies, P. T. (in press). Family instability and adolescent maladjustment: The mediating effects of parenting quality and adolescent appraisals of family security. *Journal of Clinical Child and Adolescent Psychology*.

Formosa, D., Gonzales, N. A., & Aiken, L. S. (2000). Family conflict and children's internalizing and externalizing behavior: Protective factors. *American Journal of Community Psychology*, **28**, 175–199.

Frosch, C. A., Mangelsdorf, S. C., & McHale, J. L. (2000). Marital behavior and the security of the preschooler–parent attachment relationships. *Journal of Family Psychology*, **14**, 144–161.

Garcia O'Hearn, H., Margolin, G., & John, R. S. (1997). Mothers' and fathers' reports of children's reactions to naturalistic marital conflict. *Journal of the American Academy of Child and Adolescent Psychiatry*, **36**, 1366–1373.

Goeke-Morey, M. C., Cummings, E. M., Harold, G. T., & Shelton, K. (2002). *Categories and continua of destructive and constructive marital conflict tactics from the perspective of US and Welsh children*. Manuscript submitted for publication.

Gonzales, N. A., Pitts, S. C., Hill, N. E., & Roosa, M. W. (2000). A mediational model of the impact of interparental conflict on child adjustment in a multiethnic, low-income sample. *Journal of Family Psychology*, **14**, 365–379.

Gordis, E. B., Margolin, G., & John, R. (1997). Marital aggression, observed parental hostility, and child behavior during triadic family interaction. *Journal of Family Psychology*, **11**, 76–89.

Gottman, J. M., & Katz, L. F. (1989). Effects of marital discord on young children's peer interactions and health. *Developmental Psychology*, **25**, 273–281.

Graham-Bermann, S. A. (1998). The impact of woman abuse on children's social development: Research and theoretical perspectives. In G. W. Holden, R. Geffner, & E. N. Jouriles (Eds.), *Children exposed to marital violence*. Washington, DC: American Psychological Association.

Grych, J. H. (1998). Children's appraisals of interparental conflict: Situational and contextual influences. *Journal of Family Psychology*, **12**, 437–453.

Grych, J. H., & Cardoza-Fernandes, S. (2001). Understanding the impact of interparental conflict on children: The role of social cognitive processes. In J. H. Grych & F. Fincham (Eds.), *Child development and interparental conflict*. New York: Cambridge University Press.

Grych, J. H., & Fincham, F. D. (1990). Marital conflict and children's adjustment: A cognitive-contextual framework. *Psychological Bulletin*, **108**, 267–290.

Grych, J. H., & Fincham, F. D. (1993). Children's appraisals of marital conflict: Initial investigations of the cognitive-contextual framework. *Child Development*, **64**, 215–230.

Grych, J. H., & Fincham, F. D. (2001). Interparental conflict and child adjustment: An overview. In J. H. Grych & F. Fincham (Eds.), *Child development and interparental conflict*. New York: Cambridge University Press.

Grych, J. H., Fincham, F. D., Jouriles, E. N., & McDonald, R. (2000). Interparental conflict and child adjustment: Testing the mediational role of appraisals in the cognitive-contextual framework. *Child Development*, **71**, 1648–1661.

Grych, J. H., Jouriles, E. N., Swank, P. R., McDonald, R., & Norwood, W. D. (2000). Patterns of adjustment among children of battered women. *Journal of Consulting and Clinical Psychology*, **68**, 84–94.

Grych, J. H., Seid, M., & Fincham, F. D. (1992). Assessing marital conflict from the child's perspective. *Child Development*, **63**, 558–572.

Harold, G. T., & Conger, R. D. (1997). Marital conflict and adolescent distress: The role of adolescent awareness. *Child Development*, **68**, 330–350.

Harold, G. T., Fincham, F. D., Osborne, L. N., & Conger, R. D. (1997). Mom and dad are at it again: Adolescent perceptions of marital conflict and adolescent psychological distress. *Developmental Psychology*, **33**, 333–350.

Harold, G. T., & Shelton, K. H. (2000, March). Marital conflict and adolescent adjustment: The role of emotional and parent-child attachment security. In G. T. Harold (Chair), *Marital conflict, emotional security, and adolescent adjustment: A cross-site investigation.* Paper presented at the biennial meeting of the Society for Research in Adolescence, Chicago, IL.

Harold, G. T., Shelton, K. H., Goeke-Morey, M. C., & Cummings, E. M. (2001, April). *Marital behaviour and child adjustment: An analysis across time and gender.* Paper presented at the biennial meeting of the Society for Research in Child Development. Minneapolis, MN.

Hay, D. F., Castle, J., & Davies, L. (2000). Toddlers' use of force against familiar peers: A precursor to aggression? *Child Development*, **71**, 457–467.

Hendrick, S. S. (1988). A generic measure of relationship satisfaction. *Journal of Marriage and the Family*, **50**, 93–98.

Hetherington, E. M., Bridges, M., & Insabella, G. M. (1998). What matters? What does not? Five perspectives on the association between marital transitions and children's adjustment. *American Psychologist*, **53**, 167–184.

Holden, G. W., & Miller, P. C. (1999). Enduring and different: A meta-analysis of the similarity in parents' child rearing. *Psychological Bulletin*, **125**, 233–254.

Holmbeck, G. N. (1997). Toward terminology, conceptual, and statistical clarity in the study of mediators and moderators: Examples from the child clinical and pediatric psychology literatures. *Journal of Consulting and Clinical Psychology*, **65**, 599–610.

Hubbard, R. M., & Adams, C. F. (1936). Factors affecting the success of child guidance clinic treatment. *American Journal of Orthopsychiatry*, **6**, 81–103.

Ingoldsby, E. M., Shaw, D. S., Owens, E. B., & Winslow, E. B. (1999). A longitudinal study of interparental conflict, emotional and behavioral reactivity, and preschoolers' adjustment problems among low-income families. *Journal of Abnormal Child Psychology*, **27**, 343–356

Jenkins, J. M. (2000). Marital conflict and children's emotions: The development of an anger organization. *Journal of Marriage and the Family*, **62**, 723–736.

Jenkins, J. M., Smith, M. A., & Graham, P. J. (1989). Coping with parental quarrels. *Journal of the American Academy of Child & Adolescent Psychiatry*, **28**, 182–189.

Johnson, P. L., & O'Leary, K. D. (1987). Parental behavior patterns and conduct disorders in girls. *Journal of Abnormal Child Psychology*, **15**, 573–581.

Joreskog, K. G., & Sorbom, D. (1996). *LISREL 8: Structural equation modeling with a SIMPLIS command language.* Hillsdale, NJ: Erlbaum.

Jouriles, E. N., & Farris, A. M. (1992). Effects of marital conflict on subsequent parent-son interactions. *Behavior Therapy*, **23**, 355–374.

Jouriles, E. N., Murphy, C. M., Farris, A. M., Smith, D. A., Richters, J. E., & Waters, E. (1991). Marital adjustment, parental disagreements about child rearing, and behavior problems in boys: Increasing the specificity of the marital assessment. *Child Development*, **62**, 1424–1433.

Katz, L. F., & Gottman, J. M. (1993). Patterns of marital conflict predict children's internalizing and externalizing behaviors. *Developmental Psychology*, **29**, 940–950.

Katz, L. F., & Gottman, J. M. (1997). Buffering children from marital conflict and dissolution. *Journal of Clinical Child Psychology*, **26**, 157–171.

Katz, L. F., & Wooden, E. M. (2002). Hostility, hostile detachment, and conflict engagement in marriages: Effects on child and family functioning. *Child Development*, **73**, 636–651.

Kenny, M. E., Moilanen, D. L., Lomax, R., & Brabeck, M. M. (1993). Contributions of parental attachments to view of self and depressive symptoms among early adolescents. *Journal of Early Adolescence*, **13**, 408–430.

Kerig, P. (1996). Assessing the links between interparental conflict and child adjustment: The Conflict and Problem-Solving Scales. *Journal of Family Psychology*, **10**, 454–473.

Kerig, P. K. (1998a). Moderators and mediators of the effects of interparental conflict on children's adjustment. *Journal of Abnormal Child Psychology*, **26**, 199–212.

Kerig, P. K. (1998b). Moderators and mediators of the effects of interparental conflict on children's adjustment. *Journal of Family Violence*, **15**, 345–363.

Kerig, P. (2001). Children's coping with interparental conflict. In J. Grych & F. Fincham (Eds.), *Child development and interparental conflict*. New York: Cambridge University Press.

Kerns, K. A., Klepac, L., & Cole, A. (1996). Peer relationships and preadolescents' perceptions of security in the child-mother relationship. *Developmental Psychology*, **32**, 457–466.

Kline, M., Johnston, J. R., & Tschann, J. M. (1991). The long shadow of marital conflict: A model of children's postdivorce adjustment. *Journal of Marriage and the Family*, **53**, 297–309.

Kovacs, M. (1981). Rating scales to assess depression in school-aged children. *Acta Paedopsychiatrica*, **46**, 305–315.

Krishnakumar, A., & Buehler, C. (2000). Interparental conflict and parenting behaviors: A meta-analytic review. *Family Relations*, **49**, 25–44.

Laumakis, M. A., Margolin, G., & John, R. S. (1998). The emotional, cognitive, and coping responses of preadolescent children to different dimensions of preadolescent children to different dimensions of conflict. In G. W. Holden, R. Geffner, & E. N. Jouriles (Eds.), *Children exposed to marital violence: Theory, research, and applied issues*. Washington, DC: American Psychological Association.

Locke, H. J., & Wallace, K. M. (1959). Short marital adjustment prediction tests: Their reliability and validity. *Marriage and Family Living*, **21**, 251–255.

Lynch, M., & Cicchetti, D. (1997). Children's relationships with adults and peers: An examination of elementary and junior high school students. *Journal of School Psychology*, **35**, 81–99.

Mahoney, A., Boggio, R. M., & Jouriles, E. N. (1996). Effects of verbal marital conflict on subsequent mother-son interactions in a child clinical sample. *Journal of Clinical Child Psychology*, **25**, 262–271.

Main, M., & Hesse, E. (1990). Parents' unresolved traumatic experiences are related to infant disorganized attachment status: Is frightened and/or frightening parental behavior the linking mechanism? In M. T. Greenberg, D. Ciccetti, & E. M. Cummings (Eds.), *Attachment in the preschool years: Theory, research, and instruction* (pp. 161–192). Chicago: University of Chicago Press.

Mann, B. J., & MacKenzie, E. P. (1996). Pathways of marital functioning, parental behaviors, and child behavior problems in school-age boys. *Journal of Clinical Child Psychology*, **25**, 183–191.

Marcus, R. F. (1997). Concordance between parent inventory and directly observed measures of attachment. *Early Child Development & Care*, **135**, 109–117.

Margolies, P. J., & Weintraub, S. (1977). The revised 56-item CRPBI as a research instrument: Reliability and factor structure. *Journal of Clinical Psychology*, **33**, 472–476.

Margolin, G., & Gordis, E. B. (2000). The effects of family and community violence on children. *Annual Review of Psychology*, **51**, 445–479.

Margolin, G., Oliver, P., & Medina, A. (2001). Conceptual issues in understanding the relation between interparental conflict and child adjustment: Integrating developmental psychopathology and risk/resilience perspectives. In J. Grych & F. Fincham (Eds.), *Child development and interparental conflict*. New York: Cambridge University Press.

Miller, N. B., Cowan, P. A., Cowan, C. P., Hetherington, E. M., & Clingempeel, W. G. (1993). Externalizing in preschoolers and early adolescents: A cross-study replication of a family model. *Developmental Psychology*, **29**, 3–18.

O'Brien, M., Bahadur, M., Gee, C., Balto, K., & Erber, S. (1997). Child exposure to marital conflict and child coping responses as predictors of child adjustment. *Cognitive Therapy and Research*, **21**, 39–59.

O'Brien, M., Margolin, G., & John, R. S. (1995). Relation among marital conflict, child coping, and child adjustment. *Journal of Clinical Child Psychology*, **24**, 346–361.

O'Brien, M., Margolin, G., John, R. S., & Krueger, L. (1991). Mothers' and sons' cognitive and emotional reactions to simulated marital and family conflict. *Journal of Consulting and Clinical Psychology*, **59**, 692–703.

Olson, D. H., Portner, J., & Lavee, Y. (1985). *FACES III: Family Adaptability and Cohesion Evaluation Scales*. St. Paul, MN: Family Social Sciences, University of Minnesota.

Owen, M. T., & Cox, M. J. (1997). Marital conflict and the development of infant-parent attachment relationships. *Journal of Family Psychology*, **11**, 152–164.

Parke, R. D., Kim, M., Flyr, M., McDowell, D. J., Simkins, S. D., Killian, C. M., & Wild, M. (2001). Managing marital conflict: Links with sibling relationships. In J. Grych & F. Fincham (Eds.), *Child development and interparental conflict*. New York: Cambridge University Press.

Patterson, G. R. (1982). *Coercive family process*. Eugene, OR: Castalia Press.

Patterson, G. R., Capaldi, D., & Bank, L. (1991). An early starter model for predicting delinquency. In D. J. Pepler & K. H. Rubin (Eds.), *The development and treatment of childhood aggression* (pp. 139–168). Hillsdale, NJ: Erlbaum.

Patterson, G. R., DeBaryshe, B., & Ramsey, E. (1989). A developmental perspective on antisocial behavior. *American Psychologist*, **44**, 329–335.

Rohner, R. P. (1990). *Handbook for the study of parental acceptance and rejection*. Storrs, CT: University of Connecticut, Center for the Study of Parental Acceptance and Rejection.

Saarni, C., Mumme, D. L., & Campos, J. J. (1998). Emotional development: Action, communication, and understanding. In N. Eisenberg (Ed.), *Handbook of child psychology: Vol. 3. Social, emotional, and personality development*. New York: Wiley.

Snyder, J. R. (1998). Marital conflict and child adjustment: What about gender? *Developmental Review*, **18**, 390–420.

Social trends. (2002). London: Office of National Statistics.

Sroufe, L. A., & Waters, E. (1977). Attachment as an organizational construct. *Child Development*, **48**, 1184–1199.

Stocker, C. M., & Youngblade, L. (1999). Marital conflict and parental hostility: Links with children's sibling and peer relationships. *Journal of Family Psychology*, **13**, 598–609.

Terwogt, M. M., Kremer, H. H., & Stegge, H. (1991). Effects of children's emotional state on their reactions to emotional expressions: A search for congruency effects. *Cognition & Emotion*, **5**, 109–121.

Thompson, R. A. (2000). The legacy of early attachments. *Child Development*, **71**, 145–152.

Thompson, R. A., & Calkins, S. D. (1996). The double-edged sword: Emotional regulation for children at risk. *Development and Psychopathology*, **8**, 163–182.

Thompson, R. A., Flood, M. F., & Lundquist, L. (1995). Emotion regulation: Its relations to attachment and developmental psychopathology. In D. Cicchetti & S. L. Toth (Eds.), *Rochester Symposium on Developmental Psychopathology: Vol. 6. Emotion, cognition, and representation*. Rochester, NY: University of Rochester Press.

Towle, C. (1931). The evaluation and management of marital status in foster homes. *American Journal of Orthopsychiatry*, **1**, 271–284.

Vaughn, B. E., Block, J. H., & Block, J. (1988). Parental agreement on child rearing during early childhood and the psychological characteristics of adolescents. *Child Development*, **59**, 1020–1033.

Wachs, T. D. (1991). Synthesis: Promising research designs, measures, and strategies. In T. D. Wachs & R. Plomin (Eds.), *Conceptualization and measurement of organism-environment interaction*. Washington, DC: American Psychological Association.

Waters, E., & Cummings, E. M. (2000). A secure base from which to explore close relationships. *Child Development*, **71**, 164–172.

Watson, D., & Pennebaker, J. W. (1989). Health complaints, stress, and distress: Exploring the central role of negative affectivity. *Psychological Review*, **96**, 234–254.

Webster-Stratton, C., & Hammond, M. (1999). Marital conflict management skills, parenting style, and early-onset conduct problems: Processes and pathways. *Journal of Child Psychology and Psychiatry*, **40**, 917–927.

Wierson, M., Forehand, R., & McCombs, A. (1988). The relationship of early adolescent functioning to parent-reported and adolescent-perceived interparental conflict. *Journal of Abnormal Child Psychology*, **16**, 707–718.

Wilson, B. J., & Gottman, J. M. (1995). Marital interaction and parenting: The role of repair of negativity in families. In M. H. Bornstein (Eds.), *Handbook of parenting, Vol. 4, Applied and practical considerations of parenting*. Hillsdale, NJ: Erlbaum.

Windle, M., & Tubman, J. G. (1999). Children of alcoholics. In W. K. Silverman & T. H. Allantoic (Eds.), *Developmental issues in the clinical treatment of children and adolescents*. Boston: Allyn & Bacon.

ACKNOWLEDGMENTS

The primary responsibilities of each of the authors were as follows: Patrick Davies and Jennifer Rasi were primary authors for Chapters 4 and 5. Patrick Davies drafted the Abstract and Chapters 1, 4, and 5. Marcie Goeke-Morey, E. Mark Cummings, Gordon Harold, and Katherine Shelton were primary authors for Chapter 2. Marcie Goeke-Morey was primarily responsible for drafting Chapter 2. Gordon Harold, Katherine Shelton, Marcie Goeke-Morey, and E. Mark Cummings were primary authors for Chapter 3, with Gordon Harold and Mark Cummings taking primary responsibility for drafting the chapter. Mark Cummings drafted Chapter 6. Patrick Davies was responsible for maintaining continuity and cohesiveness in editing the chapters, including various revisions in each of the chapters. All authors, including Jennifer Rasi and Katherine Shelton, participated in various aspects of the conceptualization, development and refinement of procedures, editing process, subject recruitment, and data analyses for some of the studies.

We are grateful to the children, parents, teachers, and school administrators who participated in the projects in Rochester, New York; South Bend, Indiana; and Wales. Without their generosity of time and effort, this work would not have been possible. Our gratitude is also extended to (a) Evan Forman, Lisa Lindsay, Genelle Sawyer, Kelly Salvesen, and Kristopher Stevens at the University of Rochester; (b) Janet Whitley, Claire Miles, Patricia Mitchell, Joanna Fava, and Amanda Dovidio at Cardiff University; and (c) Charles Kamen at the University of Notre Dame. All these individuals made valuable contributions to various stages of the project (e.g., data collection, coding, entry). We would also like to thank Phil and Carolyn Cowan for encouraging us to assemble these interlocking studies into a single, integrative monograph.

The development of this monograph was supported in part by grants from the Economic and Social Research Council (R000222569) and the

British Academy, the National Institute of Child Health and Human Development (HD 36261), and the National Institute of Mental Health (MH 57318).

Correspondence concerning this *Monograph* should be addressed to: Patrick T. Davies, Department of Clinical and Social Sciences in Psychology, University of Rochester, Rochester, NY 14627 [e-mail: davies@psych.rochester.edu].

MECHANISMS IN THE DEVELOPMENT OF EMOTIONAL ORGANIZATION

Jennifer M. Jenkins

In a series of elegant studies the authors of this *Monograph* test the hypothesis that children are negatively affected by parental marital conflict because they fear that the well-being of the family is threatened. By combining results from two methods, the analogue method and longitudinal, correlational designs, and across two countries, the authors provide compelling evidence for the role of emotional security in the link between marital conflict and children's outcomes.

The emotional security theory holds a unique and influential position in the literature on marital conflict. Although other theories suggest that the experience of fear is important in understanding children's outcomes, no other theory makes either of the striking claims that this is the central mechanism or that it is only information on security compiled into schemas that will be responsible for a range of emotional outcomes. This *Monograph* thus provides an original and impressive contribution, both theoretical and empirical, to our understanding of the negative effects of marital conflict on children.

The quest for theoretical specificity is admirable. The authors explicate three different theories in the literature on marital conflict, and evaluate the success of each in explaining the data. Through this process of comparison and evaluation they elucidate not only risks but the *mechanisms* involved in the links between adverse environments and children's development. Specificity in the links between a family dyad and children's representational functioning with respect to that dyad is demonstrated in this *Monograph*. In one of the studies reported, the functioning of the marital dyad was found to be associated with children's security within the marital dyad but not with their security within the parent-child dyad. Similarly the functioning of the parent-child dyad was associated with children's security within the parent-child dyad but not with security within the marital relationship. This is a fascinating finding. It builds on the attachment literature to show the importance of security in development. It also suggests, however, that security is not an unassailable unitary construct but a set of component parts based on different kinds of relational experiences in the world. It will be interesting to see where this finding takes us in understanding diverse relational outcomes over the course of development. Attachment status in adults has been found to predict aspects of marital functioning such as mate choice (Collins & Read, 1990; Hazan & Shaver, 1987), as well as the attachment relationship that develops between parent and child (Fonagy, Steele, & Steele, 1991). How will an understanding of security derived from the parental marital relationship contribute to patterns of adult behavior? What will the consequences be for the formation of intimate adult relationships if the individual has a representation based on his or her parents' marital relationship that is characterized by instability and threat, while the representation from the parent-child relationship is characterized by trust and predictability? Family research is often plagued by negative processes in families clustering together to form a "blob" of an undifferentiated adverse environment. Such co-variation makes it difficult to identify underlying processes and mechanism. Davies et al. show that with targeted measurement within specific dyads it is possible to differentiate influences that are specific to dyads, and specific to children's representations of relationships.

My aim in this commentary is to take forward the important debate on mechanism that has been raised by the authors by addressing three issues: basic processes in emotion, the operationalization of theory, and design issues.

Emotional Security Is a Theory About the Activation of the Fear System. How Does This Theory Relate to Present Theory and Research in the Area of Basic Emotions?

Attachment theory is a theory about the elicitation of fear, and the function that the infant's display of fear plays in the activation of parental protection (Goldberg, Grusec, & Jenkins, 2000). In Davies et al.'s extension of attachment theory, called *emotional security theory*, marital conflict is a specific and fundamental threat to which children are exposed. The fear that is induced results in insecurity about the stability of the family. This experience of fear is hypothesized as the cornerstone for development of long-term affective structures seen in psychopathology. This is a bold, provocative, and thought-provoking theory, especially so in that it links what is still perhaps the most important idea of the emotional basis of child development—Bowlby's attachment theory—with ideas that explain psychopathology, and that are potentially useful to clinicians.

117

Bowlby (1971) argued that the attachment system was selected for in evolutionary history for the protection of the young. This perspective of the role of emotion in interaction is also consonant with that of contemporary concepts of basic emotions, the theoretical perspective from which I work. The idea of this perspective is that emotional life is based on a few, genetically based, patterns of action and interaction (including happiness, fear, anger, and sadness; Oatley & Jenkins, 1996). These patterns have been evolutionarily selected, and can be thought of as species-typical outline patterns of interpretation and action. They are linked to more or less appropriate repertoires of response for recurring events of importance to humans (Oatley, 2000). As Frijda (1986) and Oatley and Johnson-Laird (1987) have argued, the function of an emotion is to set the brain into a specific mode of readiness for a particular kind of action.

The basic emotions perspective and emotional security theory would give the same account of internalizing disturbance. Fear is triggered by the appraisal of danger (family instability), and it functions to set the individual into a mode to avoid the danger. With repeated exposure, a cognitive/emotional structure is formed, characterized by a lower threshold for the perception of threat and the experience of fear. Although disorders involve more than emotions, there are good reasons to conceptualize short-term emotions on the same continuum as the emotions that are prevalent in psychopathology (Malatesta & Wilson, 1988; Oatley & Jenkins, 1996). Internalizing disorders are characterized by high levels of fear and sadness (Jenkins & Oatley, 2000; Keltner, Moffitt, & Stouthamer-Loeber, 1995). Both perspectives give a similar account of how exposure to marital conflict might result in internalizing difficulties in children.

So, how do emotional security theory and the perspective derived from research on basic emotions diverge? The divergence is in how anger is elicited, and in the mechanism of association between marital conflict and children's externalizing disorders. From research to date it would seem as if the basic emotion involved in externalizing disorder is anger (Jenkins & Oatley, 2000; Lemerise & Dodge, 1993). From a basic emotions perspective anger is experienced when goals are perceived as having been blocked intentionally (Averill, 1982; Ellsworth & Smith, 1988; Stein & Levine, 1989). The individual feels empowered and dominant, ready to beat the other in order to alleviate the goal block. If we remain true to the mechanism at the core of emotional security theory, then we have to explain how the experience of fear generates the expression of anger. This becomes important because marital conflict is more strongly and consistently associated with externalizing disorders than with internalizing disorders in children (Fincham, 1994).

Within the emotional security theory, and consistent with research to date on basic emotions, two points in the emotion process present themselves for links between fear and anger. First, fear may be the first link in a chain of emotional experience (Stein, Trabasso, & Liwag, 1993). Put in another way, fear is the cornerstone of subsequent affective experiences. In order to explain how threat results in disorders characterized by anger a series of steps in the appraisal/emotion process need to be hypothesized that lead to the experience of anger. For instance, children first feel threatened by marital conflict. This then leads them to feel the unavailability of their parents' support, a frightening matter indeed, as the authors of this *Monograph* postulate. This, in turn, leads them to feel that their own goals have been blocked, which leads them to feel anger. In such an account emotional security has an indirect effect on anger, through appraisals of goal blockage rather than directly through the appraisal of threat. The experience of blocked goals, however, would not have occurred if threat had not been experienced. It is interesting to note here that Bowlby's (1973) account of children's mourning for a lost parent did involve a sequential emotion process in which children experience loss and initially display sadness. When this does not result in the reappearance of the parent, sadness turns into anger. Do children feel blocked in their access to the parent?

A second process is also suggested by the emotional security model. It too is important and consistent with the functionalist account of basic emotions that I would espouse. It is that emotions serve the function of attaining goals (Campos, Mumme, Kermoian, & Campos, 1994; Jenkins & Greenbaum, 1999; Oatley, 2000). Emotional security theory postulates that once children have experienced the threat of conflict, their goal is to reattain security within the marital relationship. Emotional reactivity is both an indication of emotions elicited (as described above) and a means of reattaining emotional security. The idea here is that emotional distress functions to elicit care from others and that through this elicitation of care the goal of enhancing security is partially met. Davies et al. suggest that undifferentiated negative emotion serves this function and that children may become angry, sad, or fearful in their attempt to reinstate security. Angry emotions over the short and the long term (i.e., those within externalizing disorders) are part of this process. But I am left wondering again, why anger? Internalizing emotions such as sadness and fear function to elicit comfort and protection (Biglan, Rothlind, Hops, & Sherman, 1989; Hops et al., 1987). Anger is more likely to elicit aggression or avoidance (Jenkins & Ball, 2000). The important problem that Davies et al. have set us is whether the anger that we see in externalizing disorder is a consequence of a pattern of coping to reinstate security, or whether another mechanism, unrelated to the attachment or emotional security system, may explain this affective pattern.

Implicit in emotional security theory is the idea that security is the uppermost human goal. Although this may be true for the youngest infants, goals of dominance or status (Oatley, 2000) and goals of affiliation (Goldberg et al., 2000; MacDonald, 1992) become powerfully organized early in child development. For instance, levels of anger (Goodenough, 1931) and aggression (Tremblay, 1999) are highest around age two years. Dominance hierarchies are evident among preschool children and displays of anger, aggression, and affiliation play their role in the negotiation of these hierarchies (Strayer, 1980; Strayer & Trudel, 1984). When children develop patterns of anger expression in response to marital conflict, emotional security theorists argue that the goal is the elicitation of protection and the reinstatement of security. This may be true. There is, as yet, only a small amount of data on the goals associated with anger expression and externalizing disorders, but these data suggest a link with the goals of dominance and retaliation (Currie, 2001; Jenkins & Greenbaum, 1999; Jenkins & Ball, 2000; Lochman, Wayland, & White, 1993) rather than those of security. It may be, therefore, that over the course of development there are individual differences in the goals that become prioritized. For some children goals of dominance may come to be more highly prioritized than goals of security. Externalizing disorders may reflect such a prioritization of goals (Currie, 2001). It is interesting to note that when separate models of the mediating mechanism of emotional security were tested for internalizing and externalizing disorders in Study 2 there were stronger links between emotional security and internalizing outcomes than externalizing outcomes. This suggests that the mechanism of emotional security may operate for the generation of internalizing disorders better than it does for externalizing disorders.

To my mind, because of the uniqueness and plausibility of this theory as well as the bedrock of empirical support on which both emotional security and attachment theory set, it is important to test the mechanisms unambiguously. One direction that future research might take is to differentiate more clearly between different negative emotions. Fear should be given the empirical primacy that it has already been accorded theoretically. In Study 1, for instance, for some tests of the theory all negative emotions were combined into one measure. Future tests of the theory might maintain fear as a separate emotion. It is important to develop theory about how and why the experience of fear transforms into the expression of anger. I think that it would be of value for investigators to consider whether different mechanisms might apply to the development of internalizing and externalizing disorders.

How May Theory Be Operationalized to Differentiate Between Mechanisms That Produce Behavioral Outcomes?

A major strength of this *Monograph* is that different theoretical positions are operationalized and compared. There are now multiple theories of the way in which marital conflict affects children's behavioral disturbance but little attention has been paid to how one theory is differentiated from another. When clear and specific predictions are made, which unambiguously differentiate one theory from another, and data are collected to test predictions of each theory, we will be able to move forward in our understanding of mechanism.

Study 1 represents such an advance. The predictions of social learning theory were compared with those of emotional security theory, both with respect to the stimuli that children will find distressing and the type of distress that children show. Several findings provided greater support for emotional security theory than for social learning theory. For instance children reported higher levels of distress to threats of family breakdown (as predicted by emotional security theory) than to high verbal hostility (social learning theory). As conflicts became more destructive children described greater activation in their efforts to stop the conflict or to avoid it (consistent with emotional security theory). They did not, however, become more angry or aggressive (as predicted by social learning theory). The evidence showed strong support for the idea that children are frightened for the well-being of the family and that they are motivated to reinstate security.

As theories are usually articulated at a global level, when operationalized within a specific context there may be argument about the extent to which the operationalization is an accurate test of the theory. The operationalization of social learning theory illustrated above seemed to me to provide an accurate test of that theory. Below I outline some points of divergence between the way the authors have operationalized the two theories and possible alternative operationalizations.

Study 4 also offers a comparison between emotional security theory and social learning theory. It is argued that social learning theory predicts a relationship between marital conflict and children's aggression that is stronger in families that are more, as compared to less, cohesive. The basis of this is that children's identification with parents is stronger when cohesion is greater, and that modeling is facilitated by stronger identification. An alternative prediction from social learning theory is that the combination of low cohesion and marital conflict will lead to the highest levels of child aggression. This could be argued on the basis that low cohesion is an index of increased family-wide conflict, which in combination with marital conflict, exposes the children to the highest levels of aggression. The latter account would make the same prediction as that made by the authors for emotional security theory.

In Study 2 a different theory—cognitive-contextual theory—is the object of comparison with emotional security theory. Both theories suggest that the appraisal and experience of fear play roles in children's outcomes.

121

These theories appear to me to provide more convergent predictions than the authors suggest. Within the structural equation model presented in Study 1 appraisals of threat are "owned" by the cognitive-contextual theory. Is this a false partitioning of the two theories given the centrality of threat in emotional security theory? Self-blame is a prominent construct in cognitive contextual theory. In Study 1, child-related conflict themes, which seem to overlap with the concept of self-blame, are presented as an operationalization of emotional security theory. Is self-blame a good source of differentiation between the two theories?

My own view is that emotional security theory and cognitive contextual theory diverge on the range of appraisals relevant to the generation of affect. For emotional security theory, only appraisals about threat to the well-being of the family are relevant. For cognitive-contextual theory appraisals of threat are relevant, but so too are appraisals about marital conflict that lead to other emotions. Although in operationalizations of this theory both self-blame and threat have been prominent (Grych & Fincham, 1990, 1993), there is no reason, intrinsic to the mechanisms that are proposed, to give these appraisals primacy over other appraisals. Thus a child might see his father thwarting his mother's goal and feel angry on her behalf. This anger-based sequence of appraisal and emotion could be seen as a mediator between marital conflict and children's adjustment in cognitive-contextual theory (Grych & Cardoza-Fernandes, 2001). Because of the admirably bold assertion that only the threat of well-being to the family is relevant to emotional security, anger appraisals are not a candidate mechanism in that theory.

Design Issues That Will Help Us to Identify Mechanism

The use of experimental method, correlational design, and causal modeling is extremely impressive in this *Monograph*. Nested models are tested such that a high degree of specificity is achieved in whether particular paths are essential in understanding linkages across constructs. The measurement of constructs is exemplary. Multiple measures, derived from different informants, are used to construct latent variables. Members of this team have led the field in developing methodologies, measures, and models to explain the links between marital conflict and children's disorders.

Probably one of the more challenging issues that now faces this field is the investigation of genetic effects, including gene-environment interactions. As yet we have no studies that have taken account of genetic effects while testing effects of marital conflict on children. Negative emotionality, including anger and fear, have substantial heritability (Cates, Houston, Vavak, & Crawford, 1993; Emde et al., 1992). The same is true for externalizing disorders (Miles & Carey, 1997) and internalizing disorders (Topolski et al., 1997) of childhood. As the children taking part in the correlational studies described in this *Monograph* (Studies 2, 3, and 4), and those in all other correlational studies of marital conflict, live mainly with biologically related parents, associations between marital conflict and children's disturbance are likely to occur, in part, because of genetic mediation and gene-environment correlation.

A second factor limiting our current ability to draw conclusions about causal mechanisms is our wide reliance on cross-sectional designs. As Fincham, Grych, and Osborne (1994) have pointed out, there are many questions to be answered in a research field before the expense of longitudinal models can be justified. Over recent years, and with the advent of this *Monograph*, many of these questions have been answered. Clarification of the causal role of some of these processes will occur when we test models of change. To my knowledge, there are only two published studies (one carried out by one of the authors of this *Monograph*) that test the hypothesis that marital conflict at Time 1 is associated with a *change* in children's behavior at Time 2, having controlled for the children's behavior at Time 1 (Harold & Conger, 1997; Hetherington, Henderson & Reiss, 1999). Study 2 in this *Monograph* does not show such clear evidence that marital conflict predicts change in child symptomatology. Although a relationship between marital conflict assessed at Time 1 and children's security assessed at Time 2 was significant in the model, without controlling for emotional security at Time 1, conclusions about direction of influence remain ambiguous.

Experimental designs involving exposure to adult conflict were an inspired methodological innovation in the study of marital conflict by one of the authors of this monograph (Cummings, 1987; Cummings, Ianotti, & Zahn-Waxler, 1985). Negative effects have been shown for children exposed to live actors, and for children reporting emotional distress after seeing videotapes of conflictual interactions. However, because the outcomes assessed are not synonymous with disturbance, and the conflict exposure is not equivalent to being raised in a family in which high conflict occurs, such designs are only part of what is necessary to investigate causal mechanisms between parental conflict and children's disturbance.

Genetically sensitive designs need to be introduced into our correlational studies. Two types of design may be useful. First, adopted children in high- and low-conflict homes can be studied. Such a design has been used to investigate the effects of divorce on children (O'Connor, Caspi, DeFries, & Plomin, 2000). If the same relationships as those presented in this *Monograph* were shown when adoptive children were investigated, such effects could not be attributed to a shared genetic propensity toward the negative affect evident in both marital conflict and children's disturbance. The second kind of design involves the inclusion of children within the same family who show different degrees of genetic relatedness to one another. It is then possible to examine the effects of marital conflict, while taking account of the degree of heritability of the outcome under examination. Although traditional behavioral genetic analyses can only cope with a single pair of observations from the same family, multilevel modeling allows for the analysis of multiple children in a family and is thus ideal for population data in which full, half, and unrelated siblings may live together in the same family (Guo & Wang, 2002). In a multilevel model it is possible to take account of genetic effects while testing hypotheses of mediation and moderation, such as those considered in this *Monograph*.

The idea that difficult children predict an increase in marital problems is rarely tested in our field. Child effects on different aspects of parenting have been demonstrated (Collins, Maccoby, Steinberg, Hetherington, & Bornstein, 2000; Jenkins, Rasbash, & O'Connor, in press; O'Connor, 2002). We should therefore be alive to models of mutual influence, which allow that parental marriage has a negative impact on children and the role that difficult children have in increasing their parents' conflict. It is, moreover, plausible that mutual influence is particularly important with respect to emotional security theory. It was evident from the latent construct of emotional security examined in Studies 2 and 3 that children who are uneasy about their parents' marriage involve themselves in the marriage more. Having children intervene in the marital subsystem may make it more difficult for parents to resolve the conflicts between them as Minuchin (1981) suggested, resulting in increased parental conflict.

Conclusion

Emotional security theory, with its basis in attachment theory, provides a fascinating perspective on the mechanisms that might be involved between children's exposure to parental conflict and their disturbance. One of the important tasks in the field is to differentiate both theoretically and empirically between mechanisms suggested by different theoretical perspectives. The authors of this *Monograph* have painstakingly dissected different theoretical perspectives and provided a compelling case for the influence of emotional security in children's development.

References

Averill, J. R. (1982). *Anger and aggression. An essay on emotion.* New York: Springer.
Biglan, A., Rothlind, J., Hops, H., & Sherman, L. (1989). Impact of distressed and aggressive behavior. *Journal of Abnormal Psychology,* **98,** 218–228.

Bowlby, J. (1971). *Attachment and loss: Vol. 1. Attachment.* London: Hogarth Press (reprinted by Penguin, 1978).

Bowlby, J. (1973). *Attachment and loss: Vol. 2. Separation: anxiety and anger.* London: Hogarth Press (reprinted by Penguin, 1978).

Campos, J. J., Mumme, D. L., Kermoian, R., & Campos, R. G. (1994). A functionalist perspective on the nature of emotion. In N. A. Fox (Ed.), The development of emotion regulation. *Monographs of the Society for Research in Child Development,* **59** (2–3, Serial No 240).

Cates, D. S., Houston, B. K., Vavak, C. R., & Crawford, M. H. (1993). Heritability of hostility related emotions, attitudes and behaviors. *Journal of Behavioral Medicine,* **16,** 237–256.

Collins, N. L., & Read, S. J. (1990). Adult attachment, working models, and relationship quality in dating couples. *Journal of Personality & Social Psychology,* **58,** 644–663.

Collins, W. A., Maccoby, E. E., Steinberg, L., Hetherington, E. M., & Bornstein, M. H. (2000). Contemporary research on parenting: The case for nature and nurture. *American Psychologist,* **55**(2), 218–232.

Cummings, E. M. (1987). Coping with background anger in early childhood. *Child Development,* **58,** 976–984.

Cummings, E. M., Ianotti, R. J., & Zahn-Waxler, C. (1985). Influence of conflict between adults on the emotions and aggression of young children. *Developmental Psychology,* **21,** 495–507.

Currie, F. (2001). The relational goals of children with externalizing and internalizing symptoms. Paper presented at the Proceedings of the International Society for Research on Emotion, Quebec.

Ellsworth, P. C., & Smith, C. A. (1988). From appraisal to emotion: Differences among unpleasant feelings. *Motivation and Emotion,* **12,** 271–302.

Emde, R. N., Plomin, R., Robinson, J., Corley, R., DeFries, J., Fulker, D. W., Reznick, J. S., Campos, J., Kagan, J., & Zahn-Waxler, C. (1992). Temperament, emotion and cognition at fourteen months: The MacArthur Longitudinal Twin Study. *Child Development,* **63,** 1437–1455.

Fincham, F. (1994). Understanding the association between marital conflict and child adjustment: Overview. *Journal of Family Psychology,* **8,** 123–127.

Fincham, F. D., Grych, J. H., & Osborne, L. N. (1994). Does marital conflict cause child maladjustment? Directions and challenges for longitudinal research. *Journal of Family Psychology,* **8,** 128–140.

Fonagy, P., Steele, H., & Steele, M. (1991). Maternal representations of attachment during pregnancy predict the organization of infant-mother attachment at one year of age. *Child Development,* **62,** 891–905.

Frijda, N. H. (1986). *The emotions.* Cambridge, UK: Cambridge University Press.

Goldberg, S., Grusec, J., & Jenkins, J. M. (2000). Confidence in protection: A critique of attachment theory. *Journal of Family Psychology,* **13,** 1–9.

Goodenough, F. C. (1931). *Anger in young children.* Minneapolis: University of Minnesota Press.

Grych, J., & Fincham, F. (1990). Marital conflict and children's adjustment: A cognitive contextual framework. *Psychological Bulletin,* **108,** 267–290.

Grych, J. H., & Cardoza-Fernandes, S. (2001). Understanding the impact of intergenerational conflict on children: The role of social cognitive processes. In J. H. Grych & F. D. Fincham (Eds.), *Interparental conflict and child development.* Cambridge, UK: Cambridge University Press.

Grych, J. H., & Fincham, F. D. (1993). Children's appraisals of marital conflict: Initial investigations of the cognitive-contextual framework. *Child Development,* **64,** 215–230.

Guo, G., & Wang, J. (2002). The mixed or multilevel model for behavior genetic analysis. *Behavior Genetics*, **32**, 37–49.

Harold, G. T., & Conger, R. D. (1997). Marital conflict and adolescent distress: The role of adolescent awareness. *Child Development*, **68**, 333–350.

Hazan, C., & Shaver, P. (1987). Romantic love conceptualized as an attachment process. *Journal of Personality and Social Psychology*, **52**, 511–524.

Hetherington, E. M., Henderson, S., & Reiss, D. (1999). Adolescent sibling in stepfamilies: Family functioning and adolescent adjustment. *Monographs of the Society for Research in Child Development*, **64** (Serial No. 259).

Hops, H., Biglan, A., Sherman, L., Arthur, J., Friedman, L., & Osteen, V. (1987). Home observations of family interactions of depressed women. *Journal of Consulting and Clinical Psychology*, **55**, 341–346.

Jenkins, J., & Greenbaum, R. (1999). Intention and emotion in child psychopathology: Building cooperative plans. In P. Zelazo, J. W. Astington, & D. Olson (Eds.), *Developing theories of intention: Social understanding and self control*. Mahweh, NJ: Erlbaum.

Jenkins, J. M., & Ball, S. (2000). Distinguishing between negative emotions: Children's understanding of the social regulatory aspects of emotion. *Cognition and Emotion*, **14**, 261–282.

Jenkins, J. M., & Oatley, K. (2000). Psychopathology and short-term emotion: the balance of affects. *Journal of Child Psychology and Psychiatry*, **41**, 463–472.

Jenkins, J. M., Rasbash, J., & O'Connor, T. G. (in press). The role of the shared family context in differential parenting. *Developmental Psychology*.

Keltner, D., Moffitt, T. E., & Stouthamer-Loeber, M. (1995). Facial expressions of emotion and psychopathology in adolescent boys. *Journal of Abnormal Psychology*, **104**, 644–652.

Lemerise, E. A., & Dodge, K. A. (1993). The development of anger and hostile interactions. In M. Lewis & J. M. Haviland (Eds.), *Handbook of Emotions*. New York: Guilford Press.

Lochman, J. E., Wayland, K., & White, K. J. (1993). Social goals: Relationship to adolescent adjustment and to socail problem solving. *Journal of Abnormal Child Psychology*, **21**, 135–151.

MacDonald, K. (1992). Warmth as a developmental construct: An evolutionary analysis. *Child Development*, **63**, 753–773.

Malatesta, C. Z., & Wilson, A. (1988). Emotion/cognition interaction in personality development: A discrete emotions, functionalist analysis. *British Journal of Social Psychology*, **27**, 91–112.

Miles, D. R., & Carey, G. (1997). Genetic and environmental architecture on human aggression. *Journal of Personality & Social Psychology*, **72**, 207–217.

Minuchin, S. (1981). *Family therapy techniques*. Cambridge, MA: Harvard University Press.

Oatley, K. (2000). The sentiments and beliefs of distributed cognition. In N. H. Frijda, A. S. R. Manstead, & S. Bem (Eds.), *Emotions and beliefs: How feelings influence thoughts*. Cambridge, UK: Cambridge University Press.

Oatley, K., & Jenkins, J. M. (1996). *Understanding emotions: In psychology, psychiatry, and social science.* Cambridge, MA: Blackwell.

Oatley, K., & Johnson-Laird, P. N. (1987). Towards a cognitive theory of emotions. *Cognition and Emotion*, **1**, 29–50.

O'Connor, T. G. (2002). Annotation: The 'effects' of parenting reconsidered: Findings, challenges, and applications. *Journal of Child Psychology & Psychiatry & Allied Disciplines*, **43**, 555–572.

O'Connor, T. G., Caspi, A., DeFries, J. C., & Plomin, R. (2000). Are associations between parental divorce and children's adjustment genetically mediated? An adoption study. *Developmental Psychology*, **36**, 429–437.

Stein, N. L., & Levine, L. J. (1989). Making sense out of emotion: The representation and use of goal-structured knowledge. In N. L. Stein, B. Leventhal, & T. Trabasso (Eds.), *Psychological and biological approaches to emotion*. Hillsdale, NJ: Erlbaum.

Stein, N. L., Trabasso, T., & Liwag, M. (1993). The representation and organization of emotional experience: unfolding the emotion episode. In M. Lewis & J. M. Haviland (Eds.), *Handbook of emotions*. New York: Guilford.

Strayer, F. F. (1980). Social ecology of the preschool peer group. In W. A. Collins (Ed.), *Development of cognition, affect and social relations: Minnesota symposia in child development*. Hillsdale, NJ: Erlbaum.

Strayer, F. F., & Trudel, M. (1984). Developmental changes in the nature and function of social dominance among young children. *Ethology and Sociobiology*, 5, 279–295.

Topolski, T. D., Hewitt, J. K., Eaves, L. J., Silberg, J., Meyer, J. M., Rutter, M., Pickles, A., & Simonoff, E. (1997). Genetic and environmental influences on child reports of manifest anxiety and symptoms of separation anxiety and overanxious disorders: A community-based twin study. *Behavior Genetics*, 27, 15–28.

Tremblay, R. (1999) When children's social development fails. In D. Keating & C. Hertzman (Eds.), *Developmental health and the wealth of nations*. New York: Guilford.

Patrick T. Davies (Ph.D., West Virginia University, 1995) is an Associate Professor of Psychology at the University of Rochester. His primary research interests relate to understanding children's normal and abnormal development in the context of family relationships and processes. He is a co-author (with Mark Cummings) of *Children and Marital Conflict* (1994) and *Developmental Psychopathology and Family Process* (2000).

Gordon Harold (Ph.D., 1998, Cardiff University) is a lecturer in the School of Psychology at Cardiff University, Wales. His primary research interests relate to understanding the effects of interparental conflict on children's emotional and behavioral development, the genetic basis of children's emotional and behavioral problems, and methodological issues associated with the analysis of longitudinal family data. He is co-author with Jan Prior and Jenny Reynolds of the book *Not in Front of the Children?* (2001).

Marcie C. Goeke-Morey (Ph.D., 1999, University of Notre Dame) is a research assistant professor in the Department of Psychology at the University of Notre Dame. Her research interests include the socio-emotional development of children within the family context, with particular emphasis on the influence of fathers and the constructive and positive elements of family life and relationships.

E. Mark Cummings (Ph.D., 1977, University of California, Los Angeles) is professor of psychology and the Notre Dame Chair in Psychology at the University of Notre Dame. His research interests are broadly concerned with relations between adaptive and maladaptive family functioning and children's normal development and development of risk for psychopathology. Dr. Cummings is co-author of a half dozen books, including (with Patrick T. Davies) *Children and Marital Conflict* (1994) and *Developmental Psychopathology and Family Process* (2000).

Katherine Shelton (BSc., 1999, Cardiff University) is a graduate student in the School of Psychology at Cardiff University, Wales. Her research interests relate to adolescent development in the context of family relations, with a particular interest in the role of child gender in the relationship between interparental conflict and child socio-emotional development.

Jennifer A. Rasi (M.A., 2001, University of Rochester) is a graduate student in the Department of Clinical and Social Sciences in Psychology at the University of Rochester. Her research interests include the role of family functioning in the developmental psychopathology of internalizing symptoms, especially psychosomatic symptomatology.

Jennifer Jenkins (Ph.D., 1987, University of London) is Professor in the Department of Human Development and Applied Psychology at the University of Toronto. She is director of the Human Development and Education Program at the University of Toronto. Her research interests focus on high-risk family environments and within-family differences in children's emotional development. She is the co-author with Keith Oatley of *Understanding Emotions* (1996) and the co-editor with Keith Oatley and Nancy Stein of *Human Emotions* (1998).

STATEMENT OF EDITORIAL POLICY

The *Monographs* series is devoted to publishing developmental research that generates authoritative new findings and uses these to foster fresh, better integrated, or more coherent perspectives on major developmental issues, problems, and controversies. The significance of the work in extending developmental theory and contributing definitive empirical information in support of a major conceptual advance is the most critical editorial consideration. Along with advancing knowledge on specialized topics, the series aims to enhance cross-fertilization among developmental disciplines and developmental sub fields. Therefore, clarity of the links between the specific issues under study and questions relating to general developmental processes is important. These links, as well as the manuscript as a whole, must be as clear to the general reader as to the specialist. The selection of manuscripts for editorial consideration, and the shaping of manuscripts through reviews-and-revisions, are processes dedicated to actualizing these ideals as closely as possible.

Typically *Monographs* entail programmatic large-scale investigations; sets of programmatic interlocking studies; or—in some cases—smaller studies with highly definitive and theoretically significant empirical findings. Multi-authored sets of studies that center on the same underlying question can also be appropriate; a critical requirement here is that all studies address common issues, and that the contribution arising from the set as a whole be unique, substantial, and well integrated. The needs of integration preclude having individual chapters identified by individual authors. In general, irrespective of how it may be framed, any work that is judged to significantly extend developmental thinking will be taken under editorial consideration.

To be considered, submissions should meet the editorial goals of *Monographs* and should be no briefer than a minimum of 80 pages (including references and tables). There is an upper limit of 175–200 pages. In exceptional circumstances this upper limit may be modified (please submit four copies). Because a *Monograph* is inevitable lengthy and usually substantively complex, it is particularly important that the text be well organized and written in clear, precise, and literate English. Note, however, that authors from non-English speaking countries should not be put off by this stricture. In accordance with the general aims of SRCD, this series is actively interested in promoting international exchange of developmental research. Neither membership in the Society nor affiliation with the academic discipline of psychology are relevant in considering a *Monographs* submission.

The corresponding author for any manuscript must, in the submission letter, warrant that all coauthors are in agreement with the content of the manuscript. The corresponding author also is responsible for informing all coauthors, in a timely manner, of manuscript submission, editorial decisions, reviews received, and any revisions recommended. Before publication, the corresponding author also must warrant in the submission letter that the study has been conducted according to the ethical guidelines of the Society for Research in Child Development.

Potential authors who may be unsure whether the manuscript they are planning would make an appropriate submission are invited to draft an outline of what they propose, and send it to the Editor for assessment. This mechanism, as well as a more detailed description of all editorial policies, evaluation processes, and format requirements can be found at the Editorial Office web site (http://astro.temple.edu/~overton/monosrcd.html) or by contacting the Editor, Willis F. Overton, Temple University-Psychology, 1701 North 13th St. – Rm 567, Philadelphia, PA 19122-6085 (e-mail: monosrcd@blue.temple.edu) (telephone: 1-215-204-7360).

Monographs of the Society for Research in Child Development (ISSN 0037-976X), one of three publications of the Society for Research in Child Development, is published four times a year by Blackwell Publishers, Inc., with offices at 350 Main Street, Malden, MA 02148, USA, and 108 Cowley Road, Oxford OX4 1JF, UK. Call US 1-800-835-6770, fax: (781) 388-8232, or e-mail: subscrip@ blackwellpub.com. A subscription to *Monographs of the SRCD* comes with a subscription to *Child Development* (published six times a year in February, April, June, August, October, and December). A combined package rate is also available with the third SRCD publication, *Child Development Abstracts and Bibliography*, published three times a year.

INFORMATION FOR SUBSCRIBERS For new orders, renewals, sample copy requests, claims, change of address, and all other subscription correspondence, please contact the Journals Subscription Department at the publisher's Malden office.

INSTITUTIONAL SUBSCRIPTION RATES FOR MONOGRAPHS OF THE SRCD/CHILD DEVELOPMENT 2002 The Americas $293, Rest of World £192. All orders must be paid by credit card, business check, or money order. Checks and money orders should be made payable to Blackwell Publishers. Canadian residents please add 7% GST.

INSTITUTIONAL SUBSCRIPTION RATES FOR MONOGRAPHS OF THE SRCD/CHILD DEVELOPMENT 2002 The Americas $328, Rest of World £232. All orders must be paid by credit card, business check, or money order. Checks and money orders should be made payable to Blackwell Publishers. Canadian residents please add 7% GST.

BACK ISSUES Back issues are available from the publisher's Malden office.

MICROFORM The journal is available on microfilm. For microfilm service, address inquiries to ProQuest Information and Learning, 300 North Zeeb Road, Ann Arbor, MI 48106-1346, USA. Bell and Howell Serials Customer Service Department: 1-800-521-0600 ×2873.

POSTMASTER Periodicals class postage paid at Boston, MA, and additional offices. Send address changes to Blackwell Publishers, 350 Main Street, Malden, MA 02148, USA.

FORTHCOMING

How Children and Adolescents Evaluate Gender and Racial Exclusion—
Melanie Killen, Jennie Lee-Kim, Heidi McGlothlin, and Charles Stangor
(SERIAL NO. 271, 2002)

CURRENT

Child Emotional Security and Interparental Conflict—*Patrick T. Davies,
Gordon T. Harold, Marcie C. Goeke-Morey, and E. Mark Cummings*
(SERIAL NO. 270, 2002)

The Developmental Course of Gender Differentiation: Conceptualizing,
Measuring, and Evaluating Constructs and Pathways—*Lynn S. Liben
and Rebecca S. Bigler* (SERIAL NO. 269, 2002)

The Development of Mental Processing: Efficiency, Working Memory,
and Thinking—*Andreas Demetriou, Constantinos Christou,
George Spanoudis, and Maria Platsidou* (SERIAL NO. 268, 2002)

The Intentionality Model and Language Acquisition: Engagement,
Effort, and the Essential Tension in Development—*Lois Bloom and
Erin Tinker* (SERIAL NO. 267, 2001)

Children with Disabilities: A Longitudinal Study of Child Development
and Parent Well-being—*Penny Hauser-Cram, Marji Erickson Warfield,
Jack P. Shonkoff, and Marty Wyngaarden Krauss* (SERIAL NO. 266, 2001)

Rhythms of Dialogue in Infancy: Coordinated Timing in Development—
*Joseph Jaffe, Beatrice Beebe, Stanley Feldstein, Cynthia L. Crown, and
Michael D. Jasnow* (SERIAL NO. 265, 2001)

Early Television Viewing and Adolescent Behavior: The Recontact
Study—*Daniel R. Anderson, Aletha C. Huston, Kelly Schmitt,
Deborah Linebarger, and John C. Wright* (SERIAL NO. 264, 2001)

Parameters of Remembering and Forgetting in the Transition from
Infancy to Early Childhood—*P. J. Bauer, J. A. Wenner,
P. L. Dropik, and S. S. Wewerka* (SERIAL NO. 263, 2000)

Breaking the Language Barrier: An Emergentist Coalition Model for
the Origins of Word Learning—*George J. Hollich, Kathy Hirsh-Pasek,
Roberta Michnick Golinkoff* (SERIAL NO. 262, 2000)

Across the Great Divide: Bridging the Gap Between Understanding of
Toddlers' and Other Children's Thinking—*Zhe Chen and Robert Siegler*
(SERIAL NO. 261, 2000)

Making the Most of Summer School: A Meta-Analytic and
Narrative Review—*Harris Cooper, Kelly Charlton, Jeff C. Valentine,
and Laura Muhlenbruck* (SERIAL NO. 260, 2000)